The Franks

The Franks
A History of European Nations

Collection

LM Publishers

Anyone who wants to know the history of European nations, must read the history of the Franks. Beyond the Roman Empire, the foundation of medieval Europe also depends on the Franks whose empire evolved into the modern France and other European countries.

Who were the Franks? This book is based on historical works to present the rise and development of the Franks, and their influence in the history of Europe.

Chapter I

I[1]

Nowhere can we study the laws of national development, or follow up the human struggle for existence, with greater satisfaction and profit than in the early history of England and France. The reason is the same in both cases, and the elements of the inquiry, though differing in some important respects, are in a large measure identical. In Britain and in Gaul the race that was original — so far as our present knowledge permits us to speak of the original — was the race of Kelts. The Greeks called them Kelts; though indeed Herodotus, writing in the fifth century before Christ, said that the Danube rose in their territory, and that a people whom he called Kynesioi were the westernmost race in Europe. In any case the Kelts were in Britain and Gaul; and in the latter country, nineteen hundred years ago, they had already been pressed hard by the Germans when the Roman armies overwhelmed them. In both countries a Roman occupation gave them several centuries of comparative peace and civilization.

---

[1] Based on the work of Lewis Sergent, in *The Franks - from their origin as a confederacy to the establishment of the kingdom of France and the German empire.*

The Caesars rolled back from Gaul successive tides of invasion. The valleys of the Rhine furnished a thousand battlefields for the age-long conflict between a dying empire and a young invincible race. To such a conflict, amongst the most momentous and important which humanity has known, there was but one possible end. Before the destined masters of the world, who were to carve out four mighty empires in Europe, and to rise to heights of knowledge, culture, and disciplined strength such as even Greece and Rome had never attained, the imperial organization gradually weakened and gave way. For five centuries, and for part of a sixth, the Roman stood between the Kelt and the German, striving against fate, stemming what to him was a tide of barbarism, yet working out as he did so the beneficent laws of civil evolution, by tempering to finer consistency the hard metal of the northern races — metal which Rome could grind and set, but could never break.

In the end Rome abandoned the hopeless struggle, and withdrew from the circumference of her empire because her very existence was threatened at the centre. Whilst the last of the Western emperors and the later Roman duces were fighting in vain against successive inroads of Goths, Alans, Huns, and Lombards — whilst the Christian Church in Rome, by virtue of its compact organization, began to assume civil rule in the ravaged and dilapidated city, and thence to extend its influence to the countries which Rome had conquered and colonized, the Kelts and Germans renewed their interrupted warfare. The Rhine-Germans, no longer opposed by highly-trained Italian or mercenary legions, established themselves in Gaul; the coast-Germans broke through the defences of the Saxon shore, and carved an England out of Britain; whilst the forest-Germans, ever pressing from behind upon the fluid tribes of the western and northern Teutons, at once impelled them into the struggle and reinforced their ranks.

Thus were the new States of Europe founded; yet not by the harmony and co-operation of the tribes which made up this later Aryan development, but by their competition, and in the teeth of their mutual internecine ravages. The first Sicambrian and Chattan Franks in Gaul had to hold their own against Batavians and Chamavians, who preceded or followed them, just as the Gallo-Roman-Franks succumbed to the Northman sea-kings in the ninth century, and as the Anglo-Saxons of England succumbed to the Norman-French in the eleventh century.

The actors are virtually the same, though the arena changes; the pressure and the conquest are always from the last-formed waves of the advancing tide, from the newer and ruder Northmen, such as are still least affected by civil status and civilization.

In the following pages, we will consider the period of Frank development and predominance in Western Europe, and to estimate the Franks in relation to and comparison with the tribes and races which surrounded them. Side by side with these tribes and races we shall behold another growing and aggressive dominion, Semitic in origin, Greek in expression, Roman in organisation, a marvellous counterpart of the imperium whose deserted capital it appropriated, whose methods it adopted, whose eagles it followed into every land, and whose fate it experienced with the most significant exactitude. It is by no mere coincidence that the empire of the Roman Church, in the clash of conflict with Greeks, Italians, Iberians, Kelts, and the various Teutonic nations, gained substantially the same victories and received substantially the same checks as the empire of Roman arms.

The separation of the Eastern and Western Empires was followed in due time by the separation of the Eastern and Western Churches.

The grafting of an imperial Church on the old Italian stock led successively to the limitless assumptions, the incredible corruptions, and the eventual humiliation of Christian Rome, so that the Eternal City, as Hadrian called it, has been twice head of the world and twice the prison of its Pontifex Maximus.

Amongst the Kelts, the Roman Church has found, as the Roman State before it had found in its oldest Province, its most docile, exalted, superstitious, and faithful subjects. State and Church alike encountered in the Teutons a staunch, unconquerable foe, who spurned their control, shattered their power, and finally built up an edifice of their own on durable foundations. All this has been but the working out of the same historic laws through the instrumentality of the same peoples. With certain characters, amidst given circumstances and conditions, we have arrived in each case at very much what might have been expected and predicted beforehand.

To trace the effects of such historic laws as these is naturally more difficult, as has already been said, when we have to do, not with the marked characteristics of single tribes or races, but with the composite characters of national amalgamations. Thus it is a task of greater complexity to disentangle the motives which tend to shape the acts of the nation of Kelts, Gallo-Romans, Basques, Franks, and Scandinavians, whom we call Frenchmen, or of the nation of Kelts, Teutons, and Norman-French, whom we call Englishmen, than it is to understand the comparatively simple development of the almost unmixed people of Germany.

At any rate we have the same Teutonic elements more or less distinctly present in France, England, and Germany. Even the Franks are among our common ancestry, from whom we derive both blood and ideas. They fill a page in our island history, a volume in the histories of France and Germany.

They are especially important as having been, more than the Goths, or the Angles, or the Saxons, a hinge of ancient and modern civilization; for in the rise of the new nationalities they were ever nearest, in arms, in settlement, and in law, to the vanguard and the outposts of Rome. Yet in spite of this fact, and although the first Frank emperor, a century before the time of Alfred in England, attained to a civilization which was not a mere afterglow of Roman culture, but was in some measure Teutonic, the Franks themselves, in presence of the Gauls, the Romans, and the Northmen, were not destined to be the persistent race in the land which they had conquered. In Britain there was a conquering German race which did persist, under very similar conditions, against Kelts and Romans and Northmen ; but the Franks, who were the flower of the Teutonic family, and whose victories were greater and more striking than those of the Anglo-Saxons, left comparatively slight traces behind them in the country to which they gave their name. It is only in a limited sense that the Franks can be called the makers of France. A few characteristics of the Salic law, two or three of the customs which went to build up the feudal system, a certain inevitable blending of the population in the centre and north of Gaul, with a larger admixture of the Germanic element in the north-east,

especially in the provinces which came to be known as Alsace and Lorraine, added, of course, to the national consolidation which might never have been attained, or would not have been so thoroughly-attained, without the Merovingian and Carolingian conquests — these are the principal items of the legacy which was bequeathed by the victors in arms to their victors in religion, in language, and in such art and letters as the times admitted.

It was, indeed, the very strength of their own national characteristics that led to the failure of the Franks — if failure it must be called — to acclimatize themselves thoroughly in Gaul. They were always the most German of the Germans, in their final conquest of the Thuringians, Saxons, and Allemans, as in their early struggle with the Romans, and in their victories over the Goths Burgundians, and Lombards. Their domination in the west was largely due to the assistance of the Church, without which they would scarcely have been able to extend their borders to the Mediterranean and the Atlantic, and would certainly not have succeeded in converting their kingdom into an empire. The Church, after all, was the real victor, and the Church in Gaul was essentially Gallo-Roman. The Franks, it is true, became very good Christians; but they ended, as they began, by being essentially warriors, and they never ceased to cherish their German institutions, language, and national traditions. They were in Gaul for centuries, but of Gaul they never were, in any thorough and durable sense. The nostalgia which perpetually haunted them became with large numbers an irresistible force. When they realized that the Gallo-Romans and the northern and western Kelts could never be Germanized, and that on the Seine and Loire and Rhone they must either become Gauls themselves or be content to live amongst a race alien in language, thought, and daily habit, then, by natural and inevitable gravitation, they practically reverted as a nation to their ancestral seats.

Charles the Great showed by many evident signs that his ideas and preferences were German rather than Gallic, Austrian rather than Neustrian. He built the broad foundations of a German empire between the North Sea and the Alps, dwelling constantly in the Rhinelands, and leaving Aquitaine, Provence and Italy to the charge of his sons. A generation after his death his grandchildren divided his possessions; the empire passed permanently into Germany, and all that was most essentially German amongst the Franks tended to fall back upon the Rhine. If there was no wholesale and manifest re-migration of Franks from Neustria and Western Gaul, there was at any rate a continuing current from west to east of the elements which were more distinctly Teutonic, and which had shown themselves least fitted or disposed to coalesce with the Gallo-Roman.

From the year 843 we may reckon that the part of the Franks in the making of France was practically complete, the kingship falling (partly, perhaps, by marriage with a Frank princess) to the Angevin family of Robert the Strong, whose great-grandson was Hugues Capet. From the same year the male descendants of Charles the Great reigned in Germany alone, and at the end of the ninth century the splendid mission of the Franks in Gaul had been accomplished.

II[2]

Who where the Franks

The Franks are historical confederation Germanic tribes who occupied the right shore of the Rhine from Mainz to the sea. The name Frank was first mentioned by Roman historians in connection with a battle against this people in the third century.

The Franks repeatedly invaded Gaul, more particularly in the reigns of Valerian (253 - 260), and of Gallienus (260 - 268); and though the Romans boast of numerous victories achieved at the time against them, under the leadership of Posthumus, the general of Valerian, but who

---
[2] Based on the work of Godefroid Kurth.

afterwards usurped the empire in Gaul, yet it is certain that the Franks not only carried their devastations from the Rhine to the foot of the Pyrenees, but numbers of them actually crossed these mountains, and ravaged Spain during twelve years; when they had exhausted that unfortunate country, they seized on some vessels in the ports of Spain, and crossed over to the coast of Africa, where their sudden appearance created the utmost consternation." (Strauss G.L.)[3]

In this century, some of them crossed the Rhine and settled in Belgic Gaul on the banks of the Meuse and the Scheldt, and the Romans had endeavoured to expel them from the territory. Constantius Chlorus and his descendants continued the struggle, and, although Julian the Apostate inflicted a serious defeat on them in 359, he did not succeed in exterminating them, and eventually Rome was satisfied to make them her more or less faithful allies.

"The upper Franks extended their settlements from the lands between the Mein and Lippe gradually along both banks of the Rhine, from Mayence to Cologne; and, although repeatedly driven back by the Romans, they ultimately retained possession of the left bank of the river; whence they

---

[3] Strauss, Gustave Louis in *Moslem and Frank; or, Charles Martel and the rescue of Europe.*

were also called Riparian Franks (from the Latin ripa: bank, shore). (Strauss G.L)

After their overthrow by Julian the Apostate, the Franks of Belgium, becoming peaceful settlers, appear to have given the empire no further trouble, satisfied with having found shelter and sustenance on Roman soil. They even espoused Rome's cause during the great invasion of 406, but were overpowered by the ruthless hordes who devastated Belgium and overran Gaul and a part of Italy and Spain. Thenceforth the Belgian provinces ceased to be under the control of Rome and passed under the rule of the Franks.

Chapter II
The Development of the Franks[4]

Early in the third century we begin to hear of the Allemanni, a people dwelling to the south of the Frank confederacy. They are spoken of as auxiliaries of the Chattans in the war of 213, when Caracalla advanced through Rhaetia, and triumphed over the allies on the Main. Alexander Severus, a score of years later, found the Germans so active and audacious that he proposed to repeat the policy of Commodus, and purchase a peace which he could not enforce. He paid for the suggestion with his life in 235; and his successor Maximinus, eager to wipe out the new stain, crossed the Rhine at Mainz, and pushed far into the interior of Germany, whilst the tribes, as usual, fell back before him.

In 253 the internal weakness of the empire, showing itself at this time especially by open rivalries for the imperial throne, drew away several Roman legions from the frontier; and there was a sudden rush of Germans across the Lower Rhine, which Gallienus, son of the ill-fated Valerian, was barely able to withstand.

---

[4] This chapter and the following are Based on the work of Lewis Sergent.

This, then, brings us to the first occasion on which the Franks are mentioned by Roman writers. As we have already seen, Vopiscus in the fourth century gives the name of Franks to the Germans who crossed in 253 and the following years; whilst in the fifth century Sulpitius, who is quoted by Gregory of Tours, mentions three Frank leaders, Genobald, Marcomer, and Sunno, who broke the Roman Limes whilst Maximinus was at Aquileia, in or shortly before the year 238.

In both cases, be it observed, the invasion was made on the Upper, not on the Lower Rhine. We shall return once again to this question of the origin of the Franks when we come to consider the foundation of the Merovingian dynasty.

When Gallienus was called away from the Rhine, or from his palace at Augusta Treverorum, to another part of the frontier, he left his young son Salonius at Colonia Agrippina, with Postumus in command of the Roman troops. The general at once betrayed his trust, slew the boy and his guardian, and induced the goldiers to proclaim him emperor (260). It was whilst he was thus engaged in his own nefarious designs, and defending himself against Aureolus, a general dispatched from the camp of Gallienus, that the Franks slipped past him in vast numbers, followed by a large force of Vandals.

Whilst the latter turned towards the south, sacked Langres in Campania and Clermont in the Arvemian country, to be crushed eventually in the neighbourhood of Aries, the Franks overran a large part of Gaul, plundered many of the cities of Spain, seized a fleet of Spanish ships, and made their way across the sea into Africa. Meanwhile the Allemans broke through the passes of the Rhaetian Alps, and penetrated Italy as far as Ravenna, whilst the Goths were pushing their victories in Pontus, Thrace, and Greece.

Postumus, who had distinguished himself by permitting a greater inroad of Franks than had ever previously entered Gaul, won the reputation of a strong and successful governor before he was slain by his soldiers in 269. He was one of the so-called Thirty Tyrants who, in the reign of the worthless Gallienus, assumed authority in various provinces of the empire — some of them, no doubt, less from personal ambition than from the necessity of ruling with a strong hand, and preserving the public peace.

It is during this period of anarchy that we find distinct traces of those popular risings and insurrections in Gaul which, then or later, came to be known under the name of Bagaudae or Bagats.

They remind us, a long time in advance, of our English peasant, insurrections, and they sprang from very similar causes — constant famine and frequent pestilence, the cruel exaction of excessive taxes, military and judicial oppressions, and the general discontents which naturally gathered round any champion who strove to effect a redress of grievances. The Church was sympathetic towards these periodical risings, and in course of time she secured the appointment of *defensores* whose business it was to plead the cause of those who considered themselves to be wronged. But several centuries passed away before we hear the last of the Bagats; and the thing itself remained long after the name went out of use.

In 271 the Gallic insurgents took Augustodunum (Autun) after a long siege, when the city was sacked for the third time in less than half a century. There was a similar insurrection fourteen years later, when the Bagats aped the military pretenders, and set up "emperors" of their own.

Aurelian, a native of Sirmium in Pannonia, was the next Roman general and emperor who had an important influence upon the history of the Germans in Gaul. He was a brave, brilliant, and loyal soldier, who had held the highest commands under Valerian, Gallienus, and Claudius II.; and on the death of the latter he was proclaimed emperor by the legions of Sirmium. During the reigns of Gallienus and Claudius, Gaul was practically divorced from the empire ; but the operations of Aurelian, who successively defeated the Goths, Vandals, Allemans, Franks, and allied forces under Tetricus, another of the Thirty Tyrants, restored at once the ancient glories of the Roman arms and the ancient frontier of the empire, from the mouths of the Rhine to the mouths of the Danube.

Scarcely had Aurelian quitted Gaul when the Franks again renewed their raids, and this time with so much success that they are said to have sacked no fewer than seventy cities on the left bank of the Rhine, including Treves. The Emperor Probus, who, like Aurelian, was a native of Sirmium, and whose career was in many respects a parallel to that of his former master, expelled the invaders in 277, and taught them, by a demonstration on their own side of the frontier, that even yet they were no match for a Roman army when skillfully trained and led. Probus was equally successful as a soldier and as an administrator. He renewed what had formerly existed on the German bank of the Rhine, though for some generations, apparently, it had been effaced — the riparian *limes*, a depopulated zone of territory on which Rome in her strongest days would not suffer her enemies to reside. He also strengthened the ramparts between the Rhine and the Danube, and to him was probably due the outer and stronger wall at the southern extremity of this rampart, pushed forward into the land of the conquered Allemans — which, however, did not stand long after his death.

A distinct feature in the policy of Probus was his mode of dealing with the peoples whom he subdued, and especially with the Germans, whose personal prowess was a household word with all Roman leaders. He was not content with crushing his foes and restoring the frontiers, but he sought to disperse the more formidable of the warriors, or to find occupation for them at a distance from their former camping grounds. It has been said that Probus re-peopled

or re-colonised the old lands of Upper and Lower Germany on the Gallic side of the Rhine — which were now included amongst the increasing number of Roman "provinces" in Gaul — with his Frank captives ; and that " these German colonists permanently thrust back the Gallic frontier." That would have been a curious effect of the restoration of the ramparts, and of the riparian limes which were rather a pushing forward of the Gallic frontier into Germany.

But the precautions of Probus — which were nothing less than a return to the Caesarian frontier-policy — are quite consistent with the planting of Frank colonies, or the confirmation of settlements already made, within the secured frontier, and under the eye of the Roman garrisons, in Germania Inferior, mainly beyond the Meuse, in the lands of the Tungrians and

Texuandrians, and on the lower reaches of the Scheldt. Here their descendants were found by Julian, three generations later, and by him the more peaceable amongst them were again confirmed in their possessions.

Though the records of these earliest settlements of Franks in Gaul are very indefinite, no doubt exists as to the general policy pursued by the Emperor Probus. To his prisoners, and to such as his offers were likely to tempt, he gave the option of entering his legions or of settling peaceably in some of the Gallo-Roman provinces. Many thousands took service under him; but he was careful to .distribute them amongst his armies in different parts of the empire, nowhere leaving them collected in formidable numbers. But a band of turbulent Franks who would not be very formidable in the ranks of a well-disciplined legion might become decidedly formidable when no longer kept in awe by armed comrades and stern officers.

An interesting story is told of such a band, which had apparently been planted on the eastern shore of the Euxine, in pursuit of the well-meaning policy of Probus. According to the meagre accounts of Zosimus and Eumenius, a settlement of Franks had been made in Pontus, probably near the town of Phasis, at the request or with the consent of their leaders ; but a certain number of them, unable to change their restless habits, seized some ships and sailed away. No doubt they plundered as they went — and if they were to escape alive, and reach their home again, it would be necessary for them to obtain food, at any rate, at somebody else's expense. They disturbed the whole of Greece; there was bloodshed when they came to Sicily ; and they were worsted in an attempt on Carthage. But they managed to escape from their enemies, and sailed " homewards."

If they did not put ashore amongst their countrymen already settled in Spain, which is not very likely, they would have to extend their adventurous voyage all round the coast of Gaul, reaching after many months the land of their race-fellows on the northern shore.

Is it enough to say of these wandering Franks of the third century that they were marauders, and nothing more? Those who have told us their story would naturally not be too well affected towards them, and it was inevitable in any case that they should be regarded as robbers at large, desperate pirates who plundered and slaughtered wherever they came. It is useless to look for the virtues of peace and self-restraint amongst these hereditary enemies of Roman civilization. The Franks were sworn to enmity against the Romans, and these particular Franks had tasted the bitterness of defeat and transportation. But clearly their ultimate object was to get back to their homes again, and for this they ran the gauntlet of a hundred dangers, living, after the manner of their day and their race, by the sword, and well knowing that there was but one shore in all the world which would receive them as friends.

In the reign of Probus, all made for peace except peace. By his colonization, by his public works at Rome and in the provinces, by such encouragements of industry as the permission of vine-culture in Gaul, which had hitherto been dependent for its wine on Italy and the merchants of the cisalpine and transalpine provinces, he did his best to heal the wounds of war, and to divert the thoughts of men into peaceful channels. But the standing armies of Rome had neither the tastes nor the capacities for peace; and Probus fell by the hands of those on whom he had tried to enforce it.

The tide of war flowed on more vehemently for its momentary check, and Gaul, throughout its eastern and northern provinces, was once more the theatre of sanguinary strife.

To the incursions of the Germans were added a new Bagat, the formidable insurrection of Carausius, who established himself in Britain and seized the Gallic port of Bononia (Boulogne), and the inroads of Saxon pirates.

The Allemans broke down the wall of Probus, and invaded the Sequanian territories, where they met with a great reverse at the hands of Constantius Chlorus, who slew some sixty thousand of them at Langres. Constantius emphasized his victories over the Allemans and other German tribes by rebuilding the ruined town of Autun, and re-opening the schools for which it had already become famous.

Then followed the important reigns of Diocletian and Constantine. The division of the empire by Diocletian into prefectures, dioceses, and provinces — whereof the dioceses were subsequently adopted as a scheme of ecclesiastical government — marked a grand distinction between military and civil administration.

The prefects, their deputies (*vicarii*) in the dioceses, and the *præsides* of the provinces — of whom the last were required to be of a different nationality from that of the provinces over which they presided — were theoretically more effective for purposes of administration than any provincial authorities set up by Rome since the first century, when the proconsuls and *proprætors* answered most of the needs of newly conquered and only partially civilized lands. The spread of civilization, and the consequent increase of taxation, especially from the reign of Caracalla, had created fresh needs and difficulties, which had doubtless prompted the organization introduced by Diocletian; and, though history does not for some time afford much evidence of the success of this organization, we may reasonably conclude that it was not ineffectual under conditions which are essential to the success of any administration, even in our own days — the uprightness and skill of the administrators. The military authorities which existed side by side with the prefects and their subordinates were the Caesars (in the absence of the Augusti or emperors), the praetorian *legaty* (with restricted powers), the *duces* and the *comites*; and it was only natural that the military authority was often found in conflict with the civil.

In 325 Constantine summoned the Council of Nice, which was attended by three hundred and eighteen bishops, including Arius, Athanasius, Eusebius, (the confessor of Constantine, who, like the emperor, somewhat inclined to the doctrine of Arius), the Papa of Alexandria, and two representatives of Sylvester, Bishop of Rome. Constantine himself presided over the Council, which condemned Arius, and declared the orthodox belief of the Christian Church — that the second person of the Trinity is of one substance with the Father, not of "like" substance, as Arius held. But the battle of Arianism had yet to be fought out, as will be seen in succeeding chapters.

The short-sighted policy of Constantius, who employed Allemans to assist him against his enemy, Magnentius, had a disastrous sequel. Magnentius was himself a Frank by origin, in the Roman service; but he rebelled, declared himself emper6r, and, with his brother Decentius, gave the Romans a great deal of trouble. The Allemans performed their part of the contract with Constantius, for they defeated the rebels at Agedincum (Sens, the principal town of the old Senones). For their reward they received settlements on the left bank of the Rhine; and, in the result, we find a new story of destruction and plunder laid to their charge. The meaning of the recorded facts may be that their leaders and Constantius were not sufficiently definite in their bargain, that they did not interpret it in the same sense, or did not adhere to it, or could not control their followers. In any case the experiment was a costly one, and Julian had to pay a considerable part of the cost.

In the meantime a second Frank, who had taken the Roman name of Silvanus, assumed the purple at Cologne in 355; and the poor man enjoyed his self-conferred dignity for twenty-eight days, when he was assassinated. Between the hiring of the Allemans and the arrival of Julian, a period of five years, the Germans sacked Cologne, Treves, Mainz, Strassburg — in all no fewer than forty-five cities of the Upper and Lower Provinces of the Gallic Germania.

Julian, the nephew of Constantine and cousin of Constantius, was nominated by the latter as his Caesar in Gaul, and took up his duties in 356. He cut his way through the Allemans, who had overrun the country as far as Augustodunum and the sources of the Seine, joined forces at Reims with Marcellus, the *magister equitum* who bore him no good will, and defeated the Franks at Cologne. The German tribes had once again crossed the Rhine, and occupied or destroyed most of the Roman stations on the left bank. The results of Julian's first campaign were limited to the placing of a few garrisons in such of the cities as were capable of being held over the winter, and he himself fell back with a weakened army into winter-quarters at Agedincum, fifty or sixty miles to the south-east of Lutetia. It speaks eloquently of the disorganisation of the Roman power, and the consequent boldness of the Franks and Allemans, that he was pursued as far as this town, and besieged for thirty days by a formidable host.

In the next year Julian defeated a greatly superior army of Allemans under Huodomar and other chiefs, near the town of Argentoratum (Strassburg), fortified and held the town of Tabernae (Zabern in the Vosges), drove the Germans from various islands in the Rhine, crossed the Decumates Agri as far as the Main, and, returning, expelled a body of Franks who had occupied strong positions on the Meuse. It was earlier in the same year that he recovered some booty from a roving force of Franks, who had come from their cis-Rhenan settlements to the city of Lugdunum (Lyon).

Julian spent the following winter (357-8) in the town of Lutetia Parisiorum, which, originally built on an island, was now connected by bridges with the houses on either bank of the Seine. There was already a bishop here when Julian came, with churches and temples side by side, and monuments raised by the Gallo-Romans. At Lutetia Julian, and after him Valentinian and Gratian, resided. Here, in the intervals of war, he wrote and studied. It was here that the pagan philosopher put into writing many of his literary and critical ideas on life and morals, on Christianity and the faith of his forefathers. He exclaims in one place, thinking of the contrast between the pursuits of his youth and his military labours and studies, "Oh, Plato, Plato, what a task for a philosopher!"

It was some years later, in his satirical "Misopogon," that he recalled with affection the days of his sojourn in Paris. "I wintered," he says, "in dear Lutetia — for so the Gauls name the little town of the Parisii, a small island lying in the river, surrounded by walls. The water is very good, clear to look at and pleasant to drink; the inhabitants enjoy a mild winter, and good wine is produced. Some of them grow figs, which they shelter from the cold with straw." Paris was already a noteworthy centre of Latin civilization.

Ammianus, the historian, who was a contemporary of Julian, lays to his charge an act of treachery towards a body of Salian Franks, which reminds one of Julius Caesar's conduct towards the Tencteri, four hundred years earlier. The story may not be true as it has reached us; Ammianus was not present at the time, and he can have had no better authority when he wrote than the information of men who may have been themselves misled, either by hearsay or by the jealousy of some of those by whom Julian was surrounded.

Julian was setting out on his third campaign, in 358, and, drawing near to a Frank army, was met by a number of emissaries who sued for peace. It is said that he gave them a favourable reply, and sent them away with the presents which would be usual under such circumstances; after which he suddenly fell upon the army, taking it by surprise, and imposing terms more onerous than before. It is probable that whatever happened on this occasion was the creation of circumstances, and that Julian only did what he felt himself compelled to do. The Romans were advancing amongst a hostile race, greatly exceeding them in number; and behind the Salians there was a large force of Chamavians. They had no reason to regard the Germans as trustworthy; a Roman general opposed to the countrymen of Hermann could never hold himself safe under the terms of a truce. Gibbon says that "an inconstant spirit, the thirst of rapine, and a disregard to the most solemn treaties, disgraced the character of the Franks."

Still, it is only fair to remember that the first recorded act of treachery between Romans and

Germans was committed by the former, on the evidence of the general who was responsible for it.

In this year and in the next, Julian made a strong impression upon the invaders, defeated them in their own country, and restored several of the Rhine fortresses; but it was the campaign of 358, and the arrangements by which it was concluded, that produced the most lasting effect upon the relations between the Gauls and the Franks. Whilst the Chamavians were expelled from the left banks of the Rhine, the Salians were permitted to remain in the fields which they had virtually conquered and held from the time of Postumus, if not considerably earlier! But this concession was made to them on conditions similar to those of Probus — that they should annually furnish recruits for the army, and a stipulated number of cattle by way of tribute.

Hence the Praefectus Laetorum was added to the praefects of other foreign elements in the Roman army. It would certainly appear that the immigrants who were content to settle on the pastures which they occupied in the third century, whilst their race-fellows pushed on across the Seine and Loire and Pyrenees, stayed on and were succeeded by their children, though Postumus, Probus, and Julian had been able to clear the land of any large body of aggressors, and to check new incursions.

In 359 Julian is said to have delivered from the Allemans, in their own country, no fewer than twenty thousand Gallo-Roman captives — a fact which is eloquent not only of the extent to which the German invasions of Gaul had been pushed in the past generation, but also of the thoroughness of Julian's triumph. In the following year his career in Gaul came to an end. Constantius, who had more than once created difficulties for Julian, commanded the latter to send his best troops, Batavians, Herulians, Kelts, and "Petulantes," to reinforce the army in Persia ; and these troops, who had engaged only for service north of the Alps, revolted, and proclaimed Julian emperor at Paris. He remained long enough in the West to inflict defeats upon the Chattuarians and a new force of Allemans, and then he marched eastward to meet Constantius.

The quiet of Gaul after the five or six campaigns of Julian was only comparative, and it was not of long duration. The Emperor Valentinian took sundry measures for the maintenance of public order; but his measures were scarcely consistent. It was he who established the defensores or advocates of the citizens — not to use the term "advocates of the poor," which has a special and modern application, though the defensores were really in a somewhat similar sense official champions of those on whom the burden of civilization fell with the greatest severity.

He issued this decree on the recommendation of the Christian bishops; and it may have been at their instigation that he prohibited marriages between Roman citizens and barbarians. He was succeeded by his son Gratian, who had married the daughter of Constantius; and Gratian it was who dignified a Frank chieftain, Mellobaudes, by making him a Roman consul. Mellobaudes assisted Gratian, in the year 378, at Argentovaria on the Rhine, to defeat a German invasion of forty thousand men, described as Lentienses — descendants of the Boii, who had come to avenge their ancestors on the Gallo-Romans.

The emperor and his Frank consul were both slain a few years later, during the revolt of Maximus.

Arbogast, another Frank, of whom we hear as a comes under the Emperor Theodosius, had assassinated Valentinian II in 392, and proclaimed Eugenius, the *magister officiorum* as emperor in rivalry to his former master. But this Frank emperor-maker died in the following year, shortly after the defeat and execution of his puppet by Theodosius.

In the last year but one of the fourth century, Treves was once more in the hands of the Germans, who never ceased to take advantage of any relaxation of watchfulness on the part of the Roman emperors and their *duces*. Stilicho, a Vandal by birth — he may have been a Goth, or a Burgundian, or a member of one of the tribes allied to these, who had gravitated southward and westward from the Baltic shores through the old lands of the Suevians, for to these the common name of Vandals had been given — was dux in Gaul under Honorius, the son of Theodosius. He belongs to the line of capable Roman generals who from generation to generation were able with difficulty to stem the barbarian tide, and prolong the existence of the empire; but the Germans on the Rhine frontier were not his only enemies, nor was Gaul his only care. He defeated Alaric in 403, and Radagasius in 405; and, leaving a Gothic lieutenant to represent him in Gaul, pursued in Italy the course of personal ambition which led to his death in 408.

Meanwhile, on the first day of the year 407, huge host of Stilicho's countrymen — Germans of various tribes seeking a refuge in the West from the fury of the advancing Huns — crossed the frozen Rhine on foot, and penetrated far into North-eastern Gaul, sacking the cities as they progressed, and carrying destruction to the walls of Reims, Amiens, and Tournai. There must have been ten or a dozen fighting tribes in the country during the first decade of the fifth century ; and the Franks were prominent amongst them. We read of them at this time as far south as the city of Aries, in the neighborhood of which place they were beaten by Ulfila the Goth, who had taken service under Honorius. And it was probably during this period that the land of Hainault was definitely held by Frank leaders, who were not only warlike enough to seize and to retain their new home, but also sufficiently zealous for orderly government to implant their native Salic law in Belgic soil.

Chapter III
The Merovingian Franks

We have now entered upon the fifth century of the Christian era — the century which brings the Roman-Empire to an end, which finally breaks down the political barrier between the Eastern and Western dominions of the Latin race, which sees Italy, Gaul, Spain, and Britain overrun and appropriated by the Teutonic race, and the sway of the Church in process of establishment on the ruins of the ancient State.

Henceforth, the story of the Franks will be more definite in its character, and may be pursued with some greater degree of confidence; for now we shall have to do with a Frank people settled in a Frank land, under Frank kings — with a nation some of whose descendants, living in the same towns, rearing their cattle on the same pastures, were doubtless included amongst the Frenchmen of the France of the Capets.

We have already seen reason for supposing that the true cradle-land of the Germans who were called Franks was the country lying between the Middle Rhine and the Hercynian forest — the same country, roughly speaking, which a German of the present day calls Nassau, Hesse, Unter-Franken, Ober-Franken, and Mittel-Franken, the three last of which correspond (again roughly speaking) with the kingdom of Thuringia in the sixth century. But now it is necessary to subdivide the nation of Franks. We have hitherto regarded them as a conglomeration of German tribes, extending eastward almost as far as the confines of the Boii, and westward as far as the Limes Germanicus and the Rhine. We must proceed to draw a distinction between the Franks of the west, the protagonists of the war against Rome, and the Franks of the east, from whom the others were frequently recruited. The conglomeration or confederacy had made a single nation, the organized nation tended at once towards a rivalry of its organic parts.

Thus in the fifth century we come, in the meagre accounts of the historians, upon Franks of Thuringia and Franks who were not Thuringian. It will give a broad notion of the truth, approximately correct, if we say that the Thuringians were the Franks who stayed at home, whilst the Western or non-Thuringian Franks are represented by those who poured westward across the Rhine, in the last and most successful of the Frank invasions, under Clodion and Merowig, and founded the Merovingian realm in Gaul. It is shortly after this juncture — that is to say, in the lifetime of Childeric and Clovis — that we find the rivalry spoken of above developing into open hostility.

Of Clodion, or Hlodion, who was perhaps the father of Merowig, and at any rate his predecessor in the chieftainship of the latest immigration of Western Franks into Gaul, we know little but what is told us by Gregory of Tours; but this Roman bishop of the sixth century was almost a contemporary of Clovis, and his testimony on the point is acceptable in itself, in addition to being the best that we can get. According to Gregory, "Chlogion" (for that is how he writes the name), "a man of the highest rank in his nation, is stated to have been king of the Franks. He lived in Dispargum, a fortified place, which is on the borders of the Thuringian land. Now, in our own territories, that is towards the south, the Romans continued to occupy the country as far as the river Loire." Clodion, the writer goes on to say, drove the Romans out of Camaracum (Cambrai), in the year 445, and occupied the surrounding country up to the bank of the river Somme.

We are face to face with a number of interesting questions which are sure to challenge any one who concerns himself with the history of the Franks.

What relation did the Merovingian family and their comrades of the fifth century bear to the

Franks who had already been settled between the Meuse and the Scheldt, whom Julian, as we have seen, describes as the nation of the Salians? What is the meaning of the word Salian, which is at least as doubtful in its application as the word Frank ? Why were some of the Franks at Brabant, or other Germans settled on the left bank of the Lower Rhine, called in their own language Lite, and in Latin Laeti? And, starting with the passage just quoted from Gregory of Tours, where was the Dispargum from whence Clodion came?

In spite of Gregory's statement, which appears to be fairly precise, subsequent history has left the origin of the Merovingians in doubt. Some writers have said distinctly that they came from the Low Countries, and that they were Salian Franks, descended from the settlers in Brabant whom the Emperor Julian describes as Salians. But if they came from Dispargum, on the borders of Thuringia — where the father of Clovis sought refuge on his expulsion from Tournai by his leudes — they were not Franks of the Lower Rhine, and not Salians on that score, though they may lay claim to the term for other reasons. There is an element of doubt as to the exact position of Clodion's Dispargum ; and it will be interesting to see whether the German scholars who are making a special study of the archaeology of the Roman ramparts which enclosed the *Agri Decumates* will be able to throw any additional light on this not unimportant historical problem.

In some historical maps there is a Dispargum placed between the principal forks of the Scheldt, on what authority it is impossible to say.

Grasse, in his "Orbis Latinus," gives us two localities : (1) Duisburg, in Rhenish Prussia; and (2) Disburg, or Burg-Scheidungen, in Thuringia. Now there is a town called Deutz, formerly known as Duisburg, a short distance from Cologne on the right bank of the Rhine, and in the zone of the old Limes Rhenanus, which the Romans at their strongest kept clear of German occupants. The German name of Duisburg then or later given to it might represent Duicziburgum, or Tuiscoburgum, the hold or fort of Tuisco, the war god. Similarly there is a Duisdorf on the left bank of the Rhine, not far from Bonn. It is possible that Duicziburg was shortened into Duisburg, Latinised into Disburgum, and thence corrupted into Dispargum. But Gregory would scarcely have described this place, even on hearsay, as "in termino Thoringorum" ; for there is no evidence whatever in history that such a phrase as "termini Thoringorum," or Thuringia, was at any time applied to a district of the Belgian lands.

Again, there is a town called Dieburg, in Hesse, on the road between Darmstadt and Aschaffenburg, twelve or fifteen miles to the south-east of Frankfort-on-the-Main. It would have been within the Roman ramparts, and its position, though not in Thuringia, is in the borders of the Thuringian land. The ramparts were broken both before and after the time of Probus; and it is as likely as not that an ancestor of Clodion was amongst those who broke them. However this may be, Dieburg and Disburg may very possibly be two different forms representing the place which Gregory called in Latin Dispargum, but which Germans in their own language called Burg-Scheidungen. Now Scheidungen, which appears in Low- Latin writers as Schidinga, would mean division, or more correctly *secessio*. We do, in fact, find Divisio used as a proper name for the same place which the Germans called Burg-Scheidungen, a town of division or secession.

If, then, we recognise here, with some approach to confidence, the origin of the Merovingian dynasty, and consider Dispargum to have been a frontier-burg between the Eastern and Western Franks in Germany, we may go on to ask ourselves the further question, whether the name of Salian Franks belonged equally to the eastern and western branches, or specially to either of them. In considering this question there are certain points of departure which require to be kept in mind. The first is that we have no more probable or satisfactory derivation for the name of Frank than the statement that it was given to the Rhine-and-Main Germans from a word in the "Attic" or Chattan language (that is, in a German dialect), to indicate their character as fighting men. This, at any rate, may show that the Western Franks, Chattans and others, whom S. Remy called by implication Sicambrians, were the first to receive that name, which afterwards spread to the eastward, and again to the northward, being carried and localized along and across the Rhine, and in the Low Country between the Rhine and the Scheldt Then we have the unquestionable fact that the Franks who were permitted by Julian, and by Probus and others before him, to remain where they had settled, in the Batavian and Tungrian (Toxandrian) lands, were called by Julian and others the Salians, or Salian Franks. Why Salian? What were the limits of the Salians? And what distinction, if any, are we to draw between Salian and Riparian Franks?

In face of the difficulties created by the loose application of the names of Frank, Salian, and Salian Frank, to German warriors and settlers in a zone extending from the mouths of the Rhine to the

Roman ramparts, thence along the banks of the Main and its tributary the Sala (Saale), and to the furthest limits of Thuringia, it is impossible to claim these titles exclusively for any particular subdivision of the Teutonic van. All that can here be attempted is to sum up the conclusions which appear to be most reasonable and probable.

1) The original Franks were the representatives or successors of the Sicambrian League which opposed itself to Julius Caesar. They included the Catti or Chattans, from whose dialect the name was drawn, and whose homes lay outside the middle section of the Limes Germanicus. This view is supported, amongst other reasons, by the disappearance of the separate tribal names of the Sicambrians, Chattans, and Hermundurians about the time when the name of Frank came into ordinary use. And from the Sicambrians and Chattans the new name was gradually extended throughout the zone which has just been described.

2) The name of Salian Franks was then given, for the purpose of further distinction, to the Franks who inhabited the country bordering on the ramparts and the Hercynian forest, in which rise two rivers called Sala or Saale, one of them flowing with a very sinuous course to the south-west, into the Main, through the land of the Chattans, and the other flowing north-wards, between the lands of the

Cheruscans and the Semnones, to empty itself in the Elbe. If this be so, the Thuringian Franks might be called Salian, as well as the Western Franks whom Clodion led to Cambrai and Tournai; but it is equally probable that the name was taken solely from the tributary of the Main, and that it properly belonged to the original Franks, first known as Chattans and Hermundurians.

3) The Riparian Franks (considered apart from the Salians on the left bank of the lower stream) were those who were settled on either side of the Middle Rhine, a little before and after the time when the Western Franks under Clovis were establishing themselves in the greater part of Gaul. Their name is especially preserved in the Riparian code of German law, which has various points of distinction from the Salic and other codes. They had a *rex crinitux* a long-haired king, of their own, until Clovis annexed their country towards the close of his reign.

4) The Salians spoken of by Julian may have been Chattans by origin, as were their neighbours, the Batavians. In that case they may be looked upon as the earliest Salian Franks who obtained settlements in Gaul, occupying the country which is now Brabant The view is supported by their easy coalescence with the Franks under Clovis, and by the apparent absence of rivalry and hostility

between the two sections. There is no necessity or reason to derive their name of Salians from the river Issala or Yssel. Such similarity as the two names present is a mere coincidence.

5) As for the terms Laeti and Leti, which were applied to the Tungrian and other North-western Franks at least as early as the middle of the fourth century, it would perhaps be impossible, with any explanation, to feel satisfied that the difficulties connected with them had disappeared. Ammianus, as we have seen, tells us of Laeti who, in 356, found their way as far as Lyon, and were repulsed by Julian; the Code of Theodosius (438) mentions the Laeti in the Roman army; and the Riparian Code speaks of Icetica terra which was the land held by Laeti on condition of military service. Was this word "Laeti" anything more, originally, than a military nickname, bestowed by Roman soldiers on their foreign comrades, just as they had nicknamed other Germans Franci, Petulantes, and perhaps Burgundi, and as Romans of an earlier day had divided the Gauls into Togati, Comati, and Braccati? That is perhaps the only supposition on which we can accept any connection between Laeti and Leti. It is possible enough that Germans who paid no tribute to Rome applied the contemptuous term of lete or lite to their race-fellows who consented to pay tribute to, and fight for, the Italian

masters of Gaul, and that Roman soldiers, hearing the term, made a pun out of it, and called the more or less contented and lucky settlers *læti*. The explanation of the German term is simple enough. In the various German dialects, as Thierry has said, *lite, lide, lete*, meant a man of low rank— a *letzte* man, or, in English, one of the least of men.

We return now to Clodion, and to his expedition from Dispargum to Cambrai. He took the town and occupied the neighbouring country as far as the river Somme, possibly in the absence of any powerful Roman force. It was not long before the army of Aetius arrived ; but in the meantime the Franks had added to their exploits by capturing Turnacum (Tournai), the chief town of the Nervii (corresponding to the modern Flanders). These victories cut off the Romans from Itius Portus (Wissant), and thus deprived them of the trade route to Britain. No Roman general could sit down under such a blow without admitting that the cause of Rome in Gaul was lost. Aetius, a Scythian by birth, but a "comes rei militaris" and a consul of the empire, was by no means inclined to submit. He came up with Clodion's Franks near the town of Helena, and defeated them (447); but history tells us nothing as to the fate of Clodion himself. All we know is that the Franks were still in Cambrai,

Tournai, and Teruenna (*Terouanne*) in the next generation.

The "last of the Romans," as the admirers of Aetius called him, was a successful general.

In 425 he had rescued Aries from the Goths. In the following years he arrested the progress of more than one German inroad, and defended the Roman colonies on the Rhine.

In 434 he measured his strength against the Burgundians under Gundachar, and hurled them back from the Rhine valley into Rhaetia. Next year he forced Theodoric to raise the siege of Narbonne, and almost immediately afterwards quelled a new Bagat in the north-west, gaining victories at Tours and Chinon.

But Aetius found, as one Roman general after another had found to his cost, that the task of defending the long and exposed frontier of Gaul, of simultaneously fighting three or four enemies already established within their borders, of watching and opposing the constant popular uprisings, of dealing with the high-spirited Armorican confederation, and of repulsing every now and then the piratical attacks on the northern and western coasts, was an impossible one. Whilst he marched southwards again, to the relief of his lieutenant at Toulouse, the , Germans once more gathered in force, crossed the Rhine, sacked Mainz,

Cologne, Treves, and other cities, and swarmed over the ill-protected land. It was with, or close in the wake of, these that Clodion had led his army of Franks, keeping himself, no doubt, to the south of Brabant, where his race-fellows had been established since the days of Julian.

Aetius was prevented from pushing things to an extremity with the Franks by the appearance of another and more formidable enemy, who threatened the whole country with overwhelming ruin, and for a time united many conflicting interests in a common effort of self-defense. An enormous host of Huns — Manchu Tartars, according to some, who had gradually in the past hundred years closed in from Asia upon the rear of the migrating Alans and Germans, and who advanced slowly through Europe in the third, fourth, and fifth decades of the fifth century — entered Gaul in 451. Attila (Etzel) had fairly earned his title as the "Scourge of God.'

Eighteen years earlier he had dictated terms of peace to the emperor at Byzantium, and during most of the intervening time he exacted from Theodosius II an annual tribute, constantly increasing, to supplement the booty drawn by his swarm of locusts from the lands on which they had settled.

It is a question how far this Asiatic scourge — one of the most deadly inundations of barbarous humanity, known to history — was a propelling cause of the great westward movement of Teutons already mentioned.

The Southern Tartars and Chinese are said to have driven out their neighbours in the second century of our era; and the Huns would certainly drive other races before them. Their plan of thoroughly denuding and impoverishing their victims before they pressed on to fresh feeding-grounds might well account for a migration of centuries — extending over more than half a century in Europe alone.

Hideous to look upon — half-shaped wooden blocks, as one writer describes them, and yet more hideous in their unrelenting and destructive cruelty — they had nevertheless found or forced alliance (with the Ostro-goths amongst others) during their forward progress.

By their numbers, their spirit and savagery, their unprecedented force of mounted men, and the momentum of their victories, they were for a long time utterly irresistible. The destiny of Attila caused him to turn aside from Italy and force his way into Gaul, which, indeed, offered him at this time a richer prey. This Yellow Terror passed through the Hercynian forest and across the Rhine, devastated the valleys of the Rhine, Moselle, Meuse, and Seine, sacked the towns, and slew all that stood m its path.

At length the city that bore the name of Aurelian (Orleans) checked the advance of the conqueror. Before he could break down its walls he heard of the approach of a vast army from the south, and, knowing that his mounted forces required a more open country in which to move with effect, he fell back to the Catalaunian plains, probably between Troyes and Chalons. The bursting of this black cloud which had hung for so many years over Europe made all the dwellers in Gaul forget their minor enmities. With Aetius and his "Romans" came Theodoric, king of the Visigoths, and his son Thorismond, Franks under Merowig, and probably Armoricans, all eager to bear their part in this supreme struggle for existence. A hundred and sixty-two thousand men are said to have fallen on the field (June 21, 451); but beyond this fact, and the fact that civilization triumphed over barbarism, we have the most meagre details of what was unquestionably one of the decisive battles of the world.

Attila fled; Goths, Romans, Franks fell asunder on the morrow of his flight. Within three years Aetius, Thorismond, Attila, had all died violent deaths; and Gaul was once more the theatre of rebellions, civil war, invasion, and constant assassination.

Merowig died in 457 or 458, leaving the chieftaincy or kingship of the Flandrian Franks — or at any rate of the Toumai Franks — to his son Childeric.

The historians are not definite as to Merowig being the son of Clodion, and this is the reason why we have come to speak of the Merovingian rather than of the Clodian dynasty. But Childeric was certainly the son of Merowig.

Childeric began his reign unfortunately, setting his youthful desires on wanton pleasure rather than on the stern delights of war. He was driven from power in the first year after the death of his father, and for a while the Comes Aegidius, successor of Aetius as military governor of Gaul under the Emperor Majorian, extended his authority over Tournai, as well as over the Gallo-Romans. Majorian died in 461, and Aegidius amused himself with the usurped title of Augustus. He continued, with his head-quarters at Soissons, to fight those whom he considered the enemies of Rome, including Visigoths, Franks, and Burgundians; whilst at the same moment fleets of Saxon and Frisian boats sailed up the Loire, probably welcomed by the irreconcilable Armoricans, who never lost an opportunity of striking at their ancestral enemies. So many Britons are said to have come over at this time, fleeing from the Saxon fury, that the Armorican peninsula retained thenceforth the name which it bears today.

In the year 463 Aegidius was worsted on the Rhine by a new Frank invasion. The oft-told tale was repeated — "Cologne was sacked," and the Germans, scorning to settle in the walled town, pushed forward across the valleys, and either threw in their lot with the race-fellows who had preceded them, or, if the earlier settlers refused to make room for them, sought new habitations for themselves in the farms and vineyards of the Gallo-Romans.

Whilst the Roman count was fighting the Franks in the east of Gaul, the people of Tournai and Cambrai had grown tired of Aegidius, and had forgotten their grievances against Childeric. Their reason for deposing him, Gregory tells us, was that he had made too free with the families of his chief supporters. But when he was setting forth on his exile he had divided a gold coin with a trusty friend, who promised to do what he could to win back the hearts of his people. "If you send me your half," said the king, "and the two are united again as they were before, I shall know that it is safe for me to return." Then Childeric had gone to the castle of King Basinus in Thuringia; and Basinus would be more ready to receive the son of Merowig when he came to him with a grievance against the Western Franks. Moreover, the young guest found favour in the eyes of the Queen Basina.

One day a traveller from Tournai brought to Childeric a piece of broken gold, and he matched it with his own, and knew that his throne in Gaul was awaiting him. So he set forth at once, and reentered his kingdom. He had not been many months in Tournai before a gay cavalcade came out of the east; and, behold, it was his friend Basina, the queen. Childeric was surprised to see her — or so we might conclude from the artless tale of Bishop Gregory. "Why have you followed me from far Thuringia?" he asked her. "I have followed you," said Basina, "that I may live with you, because you are the strongest and most capable of all men. If I knew another stronger than you, I should want to live with him; but I do not." Then Childeric was glad, and made her his queen; and we can easily understand that the jealousies of the Eastern and Western Salians were not decreased by this transfer of allegiance on the lady's part.

Basina, the hero-worshipper, became the mother of Clovis.

Childeric reigned for eighteen years, and died in 481, leaving a boy of sixteen to succeed him.

Meanwhile the last possessions of the Roman Empire in the west had crumbled away. Odoacer the Herulian was in Rome; the imperial trappings which Augustulus had scarcely had time to wear were packed off to Constantinople. Gaul and Spain and Britain were in the hands of the new nationalities, and the ancient throne of the Caesars was vacant for ever.

Nearly twelve hundred years after the death of Childeric a tomb, evidently dating from Merovingian times, was discovered at Tournai, and identified by the archaeologists of the day with that of the father of Clovis. In it were found Frank arms, coins of the later empire, a gold ring, and sundry other ornaments, some of which, if the tomb were indeed that of Childeric, may have been worn by Basina. They were presented to Louis XIV., and kept in the Cabinet des Antiques. Thence a part of the collection, having survived the Revolution, was stolen in 1832, but the remainder may still be seen at Paris, a link of material fact between the fifth and the nineteenth centuries.

Chapter IV
King Clovis

When Clovis came to the throne in Toumai, the only part of Gaul which still remained under Roman organization and authority was the district governed by Roman counts in Soissons. It ran from the boundaries of the Burgundian kingdom in a north-westerly direction to the Channel coast, between the Seine and the Somme. On the west it was bounded by the Seine and its tributary, the Yonne — with an insecure supremacy on the left banks of those two rivers; and its eastern limits, beginning with the upper course of the Meuse, crossed the Aisne and the Oise to the mouth of the Somme.

The Franks had already four kings in Gaul, (1) Siegbert ruled over the Riparian lands, which lay along the Rhine from Coblenz and Cologne towards the sea, and included Tolbiac and Tongres; (2) Ragnacar was king of Cambrai, the first of Clodion's conquests; (3) Clovis ruled at Tournai, on the Upper Scheldt, over a country partly corresponding to the province of Hainault; and (4) Cararic was ruler of the last-formed kingdom of Terouanne, lying between Tournai and the Somme.

The Allemans had by this time subdued or made terms with the colonists in the Decumates Agri, and towards the end of the fifth century they penetrated as far as the Moselle. They had come in the wake of the earlier migrating Franks, as well as by way of the Upper Danube, and occupied most of what is now

Bavaria, as well as Würtemberg and Baden, between the sources of the Rhine and the Danube.

The Visigoths, early in the century, had gained a footing in the south-west of Gaul, and, after Atolf had been driven into Spain, their countrymen who succeeded them overspread the whole of Aquitaine, from the Loire to the Rhone, together with the nearer part of the Narbonensian province. Thus they ruled from Bordeaux to the neighbourhood of Tours, Orleans, Clermont, and Aries.

The Burgundians, who had followed the Goths, were settled between Aquitaine and the Alps, stretching southwards from the borders of the Alleman lands as far as the river Durance, a tributary of the Rhone which cut them off from the sea.

The possession of Narbonne, Aries, Marseille, Aix, and the other cities on or near the Mediterranean shore, was often contested, but they also fell at length into the hands of the Goths (A.D. 477).

There remained the north-western section of Gaul, the "third" and part of the "second Lugdunensis" of Augustus, which for many generations had been the general rendezvous of Keltic refugees, fleeing before the southern and eastern invaders. It would be difficult to assign precise limits to the territories north of the Loire which, before the conquests of Clovis, held themselves free of Roman domination, or even of the authority of Aegidius and his son Syagrius, the self-styled kings of the Suessiones (Soissons). Aegidius defeated the Visigoths at Orleans in 463. North-west of Orleans was the country of the warlike Aulerci, and one tribe of this formidable association were the Diablintes, mentioned by Caesar amongst the " Armoricae civitates."

Roughly speaking, it was to the west of a line running northward from the Loire, through Tours or Jublains to Bayeux (Augustodurum Baiucassium) that the descendants of the original Gauls, tempered by such Romans and Germans as had settled in their midst, asserted their independence in 383, and again in 408, and maintained it up to the time of their alliance with the Franks nearly ninety years later.

It was practically the same country which had formed a league against the Romans in 56 B.C., and again in 54 and 52, and which in the intervening centuries had been conspicuous in every effort to shake off the Roman yoke, and in every Bagat of Gallic insurrection.

The Armorican country which subsequently bore the name of Bretagne was somewhat narrower than that which has been described, being limited, approximately, by the present confines of Poitou, Anjou, Maine, and Normandy. The name of Armorica had been given by the Romans to the maritime districts between the mouths of the Loire and the Seine, to represent the term used by the Gauls themselves (armor — ad mare^ that is to say, the seaside). The Gauls had probably given this term to the whole coast, with no exact application to a circumscribed locality.

Caesar seems to use it as applying in the limited sense mentioned above; but the Armorican cities which declared their independence in the fifth century, and finally expelled the Roman authorities, included those lying between the Loire and Garonne. They were prosperous cities, strong, and proud of their immunity as compared with the more exposed inland towns. Some of them carried on a busy traffic with Britain, from whence, in the most distracted periods of British and early English history, they received many immigrants. When Clovis came he recognized the strength of the Armorican cities, and rather conciliated than attempted to conquer them. The consequence was that they gave him valuable aid against the Visigoths and Burgundians.

Such, in mere outline, was the political situation of Gaul in the latter part of the fifth century. The divisions of which we have spoken were but the temporary result of the first general scramble for the fragments of the Western Empire, when the collapse of that empire was admitted by its last defenders.

Henceforth, for many years to come, the map of the country changed from year to year. The Allemans and the Visigoths had but the shortest lease of their conquests, the Burgundians were crushed and humiliated, even the realm of Clovis was parcelled out again almost as soon as it had been pieced together, and the independent Kelts, Gallo-Kelts, and Gallo-Britons were constrained to accept a sovereign. But, after all the changes, it was the Franks who endured, who grew constantly stronger, who built up a law, a church, and an empire.

Meanwhile Clovis reigned in his father's stead, and grew to manhood, nursing the ambitions which had been bred in him, and resolved to be such a man as his mother, Basina, thought she had found in Childeric — not strong, but the strongest. When he came to man's estate he found himself surrounded by kings and confederacies all of whom probably thought themselves as powerful as he. Amongst them was his neighbour on the west and south, Syagrius, king of the Suessiones, the son of his father's enemy Aegidius. On this Syagrius Clovis determined to flesh his new-forged blade. With his kinsman Ragnacar, the king of Cambrai, he invaded the last remnant of Roman Gaul, and won a great battle near the town that is now Soissons. Syagrius took refuge with Alaric II., king of the Visigoths. The Frank demanded his surrender, and Alaric, who was not prepared to defy the young hot-head, delivered the son of Aegidius to his enemy. This was in 486, and Clovis, having slain his captive, added the valley of the Seine to his kingdom of Tournai. Paris fell into his hands not long after Soissons, and by this time, when he was little more than twenty years of age, he had under his command an army on which he could rely.

The typical Frank soldier was a tall, muscular man, well-strung to his work, and inured by constant training in war and the chase. Light of complexion until the weather had tanned his face and arms, with red or yellow hair and moustache — the king and his *leudes* and *antrustions* wearing two long plaits which reached the waist — he must have been as handsomely set-up as he was prompt and vigorous in fight. His close-fitting vest, lined outside with the furred skins of animals, gradually gave way to a coat of mail, under which a short-sleeved tunic hung down to his knees. His leather shoes were secured by long strips which crossed each other round the shins and above the knees; and he carried a lance (originally the framea, headed with a flat iron tip, varying in shape), javelins, a battle-axe, a dagger, a double-edged sword, and a round, oval, or straight-edged shield, with its boss drawn out to a point.

Most of the German fighting men were of this stamp, but the event proved that none of them were stronger, braver, or more formidable when their blood was up than the Franks. To say that they were cruel and bloodthirsty is to speak a commonplace.

In that respect they scarcely differed from the Romans, who had trained or sharpened their aptitude for war. It was in the Roman army itself that they had learned the arts of discipline, the traditions of soldierly drill and camp-life, which converted a brave man into a hardened legionary. There is abundant evidence that the Riparian, the Sicambrian, the Chattan, the Salian Frank had learned all that Rome had to teach, and learned it better than the Alleman, the Goth, the Burgundian, or the Langobard. They had learned, in short, how to create an army out of a crowd of men. The swarms by whom Caesar used to find himself surrounded were formidable enough, even when they had nothing to oppose to the Roman legions except their bare bodies and a handful of darts; but when the enervated Italian began to stay at home and fill the ranks with trained barbarians, he was simply creating the instrument which was to destroy him.

Gregory of Tours gives us a striking picture of Clovis and his *leudes* at the time when the Franks were overrunning the kingdom of Syagrius, which incidentally shows us how the old habits of the raiding barbarian had begun to be controlled and held in hand by the spirit of a disciplined army and the authority of a military king.

About this time, says Gregory, many of the churches had been plundered by the army of Clovis, for he was still sunk in his grievous errors. From one church these enemies of the faith had carried off a bowl of remarkable size and beauty, as well as other beautiful vessels used in the services of the church. Therefore the bishop sent a messenger to the king, beseeching that, if he could not prevail to have any of the other sacred vessels restored, at any rate the bowl belonging to his church might be given back to him. And the king said to the speaker: "Follow me to Suessiones, for there all the treasure which has been taken is to be parcelled out, and, if this vessel falls by lot to me, I will do as the Papa wishes." And when they came to Suessiones, and all the booty had been arranged in the midst, before Clovis and his warriors, the king said to his *leudes* : "I beg only this thing of my brave warriors, that they will not refuse to give me yonder bowl, over and above what falls to me by lot."

And the *leudes* said that they and everything belonged to the king, that he must do and take what seemed good to him, for no man could withstand him.

But one foolish fellow, who was greedy and head-strong, raised his battle-axe and smote the bowl, and said, "Nought shalt thou have, beyond whatever the lot may give thee !" And they were all amazed at these words, but the . king governed himself. And when he had received the bowl he gave it to the messenger, but he nursed in his heart the memory of that insult. And when the year was at an end he ordered the whole army to assemble for a parade of arms. And as he went slowly round the ranks he came to him who had smitten the bowl. And he said to him, "No man has arms so ill cared for as thou. Neither spear nor sword nor hatchet is fit for use! "And he seized his hatchet and flung it on the ground. And when the man was stooping to pick it up again the king raised his two hands and buried his own blade in the warriors skull. "Thus didst thou," said he, "to that bowl at Suessiones."

Within the next year or two Clovis took up the ancestral quarrel of the Western Franks — a quarrel which may never yet have come to a violent breach, and which may have amounted to a mere secession of one branch of the Salians from the other branch, to a mere division of the land on the east and west of the Scheidungen-burg. Jealousy there must have been, as a natural consequence, and the jealousy had turned into bad blood when Basina left her husband's castle to follow her "strongest man" into the plains of Gaul. So the son of the errant hero-worshipper sent or led his victorious army, swollen with levies from the Riparian Franks, and attacked the Eastern Salians.

We have but a scanty record of this expedition. Gregory of Tours, who possibly knew more about it than he has told us, is mainly concerned with the relations between Church and State in Gaul, and is at this point eager to come to the all-important fact of the conversion of Clovis.

How far was this quarrel between Western and Eastern Franks, or between Franks and Thuringians, hereditary? It is impossible to be precise in tracing the pedigree of Franks to Chattans, or of Thuringians to Hermundurians, and it may be only fanciful to refer the reader to a story which Tacitus relates of the year 58. "The same summer a great battle was fought between the Hermunduri and the Chatti, both forcibly claiming a river which produced salt in plenty, and bounded their territories. They had not only a passion for settling every question by arms, but also a deep-rooted superstition that such localities are especially near to heaven, and that mortal prayers are nowhere more attentively heard by the gods. It is, they think, through the bounty of divine power that in that river and in those forests salt is produced, not, as in other countries, by the drying up of an overflow of the sea, but by the combination of two opposite elements, fire and water, when the latter has been poured over a burning pile of wood. The war was a success for the Hermunduri, and the more disastrous to the Chatti because they had devoted, in the event of victory, the enemy's army to Mars and Mercury, a vow which consigns horses, men, everything, indeed, on the vanquished side to destruction. And so the hostile threat recoiled on themselves.'"

Salt and potash are still plentiful in Saxony, to which the Elbe Sala is somewhat nearer than the Main Sala; but it is most probable that the latter river is the one indicated by Tacitus as a boundary between the Chattans and the Hermundurians.

The marriage of Clovis to Clotilda (Chrotechilde), the Burgundian, is compact with romance — and let us understand at once that the future history of the Franks is as full of romance as the most glowing imagination could desire. The romance of the Middle Ages is largely Teutonic or Scandinavian, and, more than anything else, it is Frank, or Gallo-Frank and Burgundian, not Roman, not even Gothic or Alleman, or Thuringian, or even Saxon in any large degree, but by great preponderance Frank and Norse.

Gundachar, king of the Burgundians, son of Athanaric, whom the Christians had had no cause to love, was converted in 430. He had suffered at the hand of Aetius, as well as of Attila ; but, after he had embraced Christianity (though in its heretical form), and after the defeat of Attila, he established his dominion in the south-east of Gaul. He left four sons, Gundobald, Godegisil, Chilperic, and Godomar, whereof the two elder brothers were sorry rogues, even if judged by the standard of their time. Gundobald slew his brother Chilperic, tied a stone round the neck of his wife and drowned her, and would have slain her two daughters if they had not been hidden by their friends. Emissaries of Clovis saw the maiden Clotilda, and told their master of her beauty, whereupon the king of the

Franks demanded her in marriage. Gundobald, who by this time was king, and had recently extended his dominions to Aix and Marseille, dare not deny his powerful neighbour. Now Clovis already had a son Theodoric, who was the child of a pagan wife, but when he saw Clotilda he loved her very deeply, as all his acts sufficiently show.

Clotilda was very young when she was married; but, however young she may have been, she was a good Christian, and she made up her mind to proselytise the king of the Franks. Fortunately for the Church, although she sprang from a family of rank Arians, she was an Orthodox Christian — a fact easily accounted for if the friends who rescued her from her uncle were themselves Orthodox. Now there was an Orthodox bishop of Tournai. There had been a bishop of Paris, under the archbishop of Sens, for a century or two; but the archives of the bishopric of Tournai date the first appointment in 487, and the second in the following year — that is to say, at the moment when Clovis was reducing the kingdom of Soissons. Clotilda's first son was Ingomer, and she had him baptized at Tournai, as likely as not by Bishop Eleutherios. Almost immediately the child sickened and died. Clovis reproached his wife with her confidence in the God of the Christians. "You have often told me," he said, "that my gods can do nothing for me —that they are but wood, or stone, or iron. Your God you think all-mighty, one that hears and answers those who believe in him. You took our son and caused him to be baptized in the church of the Christians, and behold, it has killed him. My gods are angry, and yours cannot help us." Clotilda answered him like a saint. "I bear up against my sorrow," she said, "because I believe in the wisdom and goodness of the true God. Ingomer is with the whitest angels in heaven."

As for Clovis, he was engrossed at this time in a fruitless effort to subdue the Armoricans, who made as good a stand against him as they had made against former enemies — for a coastwise people is rarely subdued until battle has been waged by sea as well as by land. About the end of 495, or the beginning of 496, Clotilda had her second boy.

Of course he was christened, just as Ingomer had been, and she called him Chlodomer. As bad luck would have it, Chlodomer sickened too; and Clovis began to storm again, saying that the God of the Christians was worse than useless. But Clotilda told him that she was praying for the child; and she prayed, and he recovered.

The king was dubious, but not convinced. Full of joy at the recovery of his son, he set out on his expedition against the Allemans, at the head of a large army of Franks, who were not all his own particular subjects. At any rate he was accompanied by Siegbert, ruler of the Riparians, who held his court at Cologne, and who in this battle was dangerously wounded in the foot. The campaign was by no means easily won, though Clovis was successful in the end, and the South Germans were finally driven out of Gaul. Clovis pursued them into their own land, and his victory was so complete that they did not care to try conclusions with him again.

It was at a critical moment of his chief engagement with the Allemans near Tolbiac that Clovis, finding himself hard pressed, raised his eyes to heaven, as Gregory imagines the scene, being pricked to the heart and weeping sore; and he said : "Jesus Christ, whom Clotilda declares to be the son of the living God, who art said to give help to those in trouble and victory to those who trust in Thee, I earnestly pray for Thy succour. If Thou wilt grant me the victory over these foes, and if I behold the strength that this people who are called after Thy name declare that they have found in Thee, then I will believe in Thee, and will be baptized in Thy name. For I have called on my gods, but they are far from helping me, so that I think they have no power at all, seeing that they do not aid such as render them obedience. Now do I call on Thee, with good will to believe in Thee, so that Thou save me from mine enemies." And whilst he was yet speaking, the Allemans lost their courage and fled.

When the conqueror returned to his home, and told Clotilda that he had called upon her God in the day of battle, that his prayer had been heard, and that he was ready to be baptized, there was great rejoicing. It was determined to have an imposing ceremonial, such as, even in those days, the bishops in their handsome and well-found churches were able to provide. The church at Tournai was not fine enough; moreover Tournai was not sufficiently central. It was different with Reims, the old capital of the Remi, already important before the Romans came, and especially important to them as the strongest place west-ward of Treves, when Augusta Treverorum was the capital city of Northern Gaul. Reims, as the ecclesiastical writers say, was the metropolitan bishopric of Western Belgica, the diocese created by Diocletian and adopted by the Christian Church; whilst Tournai, Cambrai, Terouanne and Soissons were amongst the eleven sees subordinated to it.

Here there was a venerable bishop, Remigius or Remy, the seventh of his line destined for canonisation as a saint It was therefore at Reims that Clovis, by direction of the Church, was to be baptized. All the bishops in his dominions were apparently summoned to attend; the church was richly decorated and censed; there would be a magnificent spectacle for a people who loved magnificent spectacles, and gay processions in the streets, both religious and military. For Clovis was attended by three thousand of his picked soldiers, who were to be baptized on the same day, the first sheaves of the harvest which the Church now set itself to reap.

Bishop Remy had the dignity of his order, as well as the bearing of the saint and the imagination of the poet. Gregory gives us no more than the opening sentences of his address— or perhaps this was all that he said to the fierce young warrior who strode up to the font, stripped of his mail and his casque, and clad in a long tunic of white : — "*Mitis depone colla Sicamber : adora quod i incendisti, incende quod adorasti*" — "Worship what you have burned, bum what you have worshipped." And so the most powerful *rex crinitus* of the Western Franks became a professing Orthodox Christian — won over by his personal interest, no doubt, but also by his hour of agonizing prayer on the field of Tolbiac, and, perhaps most of all, by the love and the adroitness of Clotilda.

By the cruel irony of coincidence, Albofleda, the sister of Clovis, who was baptised at the same time with her brother, died not many days afterwards. It is to be hoped that the king did not see in this misfortune, as he saw in the death of Ingomer, the avenging wrath of the gods of his ancestors. Apparently a little before this time, the other sister of Clovis, Augofleda, was married to Theodoric, king of the Ostrogoths, a tolerant Arian in religion, and naturally more attracted than his brother-in-law to the civilization of Rome.

It may or may not have been the firstfruits of his conversion that, in the following year, Clovis offered terms of alliance to the Armorican cities. No doubt he found himself partly dependent upon them for supplies of various kinds, and recognized the difficulty of their complete subjugation. Moreover he had other designs in hand ; for it was evident that he nursed the ambition of ruling over the whole of Gaul, and the Burgundians and Visigoths were already in constant dread of his attack. But, before we deal with the remaining years of the life of Clovis, it will be well to glance at the position now held by the Gallican Church, and by the Christian Church in general, for this will assist us to understand the narrative which follows.

Chapter V

Conquests of Christianity

The baptism of Clovis, which implied the general conversion of the Franks to Christianity, set the crown on a century of striking successes for the Western Church. The Goths had been partially Christianized in Moesia, and their migration into Gaul had established a State in the south-west of that country which acknowledged and protected the new faith. The Burgundians in the south-east were also Christians. The Gallo-Romans had mostly followed the line taken in the preceding century by the Christian emperors, and, though since the time of Constantine there had been more than one Augustus who either clung openly to the pagan creed, like Julian, or treated Christian and pagan with impartial indifference, the Christian religion was rapidly extending, and the secular imperium had practically given place to the spiritual. The Kelts readily embraced the faith of Christ; there was a bishop of Nantes in the third century, though Rennes, the chief town of Brittany, was behind its sister-city in this respect. The Armoricans traded with Ireland, and early in the fifth century St. Patrick, a missionary bishop from the Breton Church, crossed the seas and (so the fable runs) converted a new kingdom.

Humanly speaking, the success of the Church in building up its great authority, not merely over monarchs and people, but also between different monarchs and different peoples, was due in a large measure to its perfect organization in the midst of so much that was disorganized. The bishops and their clergy knew their own minds, and their ambitions were directed, as a rule, to a single object, external to themselves, whereas the organization of the State constantly varied, and the ambitions of *Caesars, duces, praetors, comites*, and fiscal officers were frequently, if not usually, centred in their personal interests. Thus, both on spiritual and on secular grounds, it was inevitable that Christianity, implanted in the decaying empire, should strike its roots deep in the soil, and grow with phenomenal rapidity.

So rapidly did it grow that already in the fourth and fifth centuries, before the last Augustus of the imperial State had worn the purple and laid it aside, the Christian bishops afforded many striking examples of that august imperiousness which distinguished the popes and bishops of a later day. None of these instances is more striking than the story of the penance of Theodosius the Great Theodosius was associate emperor with Gratian, and afterwards sole Emperor of the East; he defeated the Goths in 382, and the usurper

Maximus five years later. Whilst he was living at Milan, in 390, some local trouble broke out at Thessalonika, and a few soldiers were slain by the rioters. The emperor sent an armed force, who would of course be mainly barbarians, with orders to stamp out the disaffection.

The citizens were tempted into the circus by an exceptionally brilliant spectacle; and, when the place was as full as it would hold, the soldiers secured the entrances and slaughtered all the spectators, to the number of seven thousand or more. Theodosius made no secret of his responsibility for this act of retribution; but when he went to worship at the church of Ambrose, the archbishop of Milan, Ambrose met him in the porch, and refused to admit him except as a penitent. So Theodosius (who had doubtless been warned by the archbishop of what he intended to do) put off his imperial robes, assumed the white garb of penitence, and openly confessed his sin before the congregation. As a penance he was excluded from communion for a period of eight months. Thus, and thus early, did the Christian , Church assert the supremacy of its authority over the most mighty potentates.

The gradual assertion of the spiritual dominion over the hearts of Romans and barbarians alike, the great part which was played by men like Leo of

Rome, whose eloquence and personal dignity sufficed to deliver the capital of the empire out of the hands of Attila and his Huns, the conversion of ruthless warriors like Clovis, combine to impress us with a sense of the sublime confidence and inspired courage of these leaders of a faith which was still young, still despised by perhaps a majority of intellectual men and barely at this time recovering from the last of the general persecutions. It is true that there was often much subtlety united with the confidence and courage by which these victories were obtained. It was the vision of an angel by Leo's side which had turned the superstitious heart of Attila; it was a coincidence interpreted as a miracle which had persuaded Clovis that the God of Clotilda would fight his battles for him. But the builders of the Church were Italians, who had not ceased to be Italians when they became Christians; and it must be admitted that the means which they sometimes adopted to extend the frontier of the faith remind one rather of the pagan whose cunning had always supplemented his physical prowess, than of the guileless disciple of Christ.

We have been speaking of the ecclesiastics who concerned themselves, by choice or necessity, with the tortuous ways and methods of statecraft, with kings and warriors who were not to be won for the new faith by mere admonitions, or even by the championship of civil and social rights. It was by such means that the humbler converts had been won, and still continued to be won. The slavery of the slaves, the sufferings of the poorest taxpayers, the misery of the unsettled and fugitive population which filled the ranks of successive Bagats, were a soil prepared beforehand for the husbandry of the Christian preachers, and their harvest was already great when the first barbarian king underwent the rite of baptism. It was the bishops, as we have said, who secured from Valentinian the appointment of the *defensores* ; it was to them, as being ever ready to hear and to advise, that all who had grievances arising out of the abuse of the civil powers naturally brought their complaints.

Socially, spiritually, and intellectually, the Gallic Church stood prominent in the Christian commonwealth, long before the conversion of Clovis. Just as Roman letters and the pagan culture had been cherished in Gaul, from the older Province to the northern sea, from the birthplace of Ausonius to the home of his maturer years, even when they languished at Rome and in Middle Italy, so the Church in Gaul was stronger and purer, and more free from widespread heresies, than any other of the Western Churches. From the Eternal City, as Hadrian had called her in the palmy days of empire, from Rome thrice sacked, and often menaced with destruction, the bishops repeatedly appealed to the civil power in Gaul for the defence of the Church against her foes. Thus Sidonius, bishop of Clermont, who died in 488, addressed a Latin poetical epistle to Euaric, king of the Visigoths, urging him to go to the protection of Rome during the visitation of the Vandals.

The conversion of Clovis, after his earlier victories had been achieved, and when the probability of still greater conquests must have been apparent to all observers, naturally inspired the then bishop of Rome, Gregory the Great, with definite hopes of championship from the young and vigorous nationality of the Franks. Clovis was hailed as "rex Christianissimus." Avitus, bishop of Vienne, in what was now Burgundian land, wrote to Clovis excusing himself for not having attended the ceremony of his baptism ; and he ended in this strain : "This alone I beseech you, that you will spread amongst the nations around you the light which you have received. Sow the seeds of faith from the garner of your heart, and do not hesitate to send missions to other states, that they may advance the cause of that God who has so greatly exalted you. May you shine forever, by your crown on those who are present with you, by the glory of your name on those who are absent. We sympathize with your joy, and, so often as you fight in those lands, we conquer."

Whilst these half-converted Teutons fought their way to a fuller civilization and a purer Christianity, the sympathies of the Church were inevitably with the Orthodox rulers, and against the unorthodox.

For it was clearly understood in those days that the orthodoxy of the Church could only be established by force of arms ; that the faith as they saw it at Constantinople and at Rome, the faith in the equal godhead of the three Persons of the Trinity, which Arius had denied at Alexandria, for which Athanasius had contended against Arius, and which the Council of Nice had confirmed and defined in 325, would perhaps never be perpetuated unless Rome could enlist the strongest nationalities in her service, and unless she was bold enough to bid them draw the sword, and shed the blood of the heretics. Rome saw, with a clearness of intellectual vision which did more than anything else to establish her predominance amongst the Christian Churches, that the temptation to say, "There is only One God, and the Holy Ghost is His emanation, and Jesus is only His prophet," would evermore be almost irresistible to simple minds. But at the same time she saw that, in that case, these same simple minds would go on to conclude that God was vague and impersonal, that Jesus was only human and therefore fallible, and that his philosophy was as open for discussion as that of Plato. Therefore, thirdly, Rome saw that the only chance of maintaining the saving faith in Christ unimpaired and effectual for all ages was to establish at once, and once for all, the full doctrine of the Trinity in Unity — that God is One, that Christ is one with Him, and that it is a blasphemy to speak of the procession of the Holy Ghost from God, and not from Christ also.

This was the foresight of Rome, and this is her distinctive part in the building of the Christian creed. For a long time, for nearly two centuries, the issue between Arianism and Roman orthodoxy was in doubt. To the beginning of the sixth century it must have appeared to many that the gospel as interpreted by Arius, as accepted even by Councils which had not yet been discredited, would eventually prevail. The danger apparent in Africa seemed to be even greater in Northern and Western Europe, for the Germanic nations were almost unanimous in favour of the heresy. The Goths adopted the views of Arius, and so did the Burgundians and the Vandals. The earlier Teutons, as Tacitus tells us, had had the notion of one original god, with human attributes, though they held that Tuisco sprang from the earth instead of from heaven. They more easily grasped the idea of divine unity than of divine triunity. However this may have been, it is necessary to remember that the invaders who overran or governed Southern Europe in the fifth century, so far as they were of European origin — Odoacer, Theodoric, Alaric, Gaiseric, Gundachar — were Arians, whilst the Churches of Greece, Italy, and Gaul were Orthodox. It was not without influence on subsequent events that Athanasius in his banishment lived and taught at Treves, where Hilary of Aries was amongst his disciples. For when Romanised Gaul was overrun by the barbarian hosts, she won this victory in her defeat for Christianized Rome, that the strongest nation of Europe became an Orthodox Power.

As we have already seen, these European invaders — we may exclude the Huns and other Asiatic races from consideration — were by no means intractable when they had secured a settlement in Roman or Romanised lands. They adopted Christianity, they respected and imitated the Roman civilization, some more readily than others, but all of them sooner or later. The Goths especially grew comparatively mild and tolerant in a few generations, and began to apply themselves to the arts of peace. But if the ancient animosity between Roman and Teuton was dying out, the old fighting instincts of the Central and Western Germans, continually reinforced or stimulated from the north, by no means tended to disappear. The enmities were modified in some respects, and became more sectional in their manifestation, but they gained in intensity what they lost in extent. In the period of transition which we are now considering, the translated nations, having no longer a common Roman enemy to contend against, contended with each other; and they fought, not as of old, for their liberty, but for one form or other of the Christianity which they had embraced.

This is an important fact in the history of the Franks. They came into Gaul, it is true, well-equipped for the part which they had to play, the most keen in war, the most resolute in purpose, the most ambitious of rule, amongst the German peoples.

They had been the foremost opponents of Rome for five centuries, they were the first settlers in Gaul, and they were superior in arms, as the event proved, to all their competitors. But from the end of the fifth century they had an additional sanction and encouragement in the favour of the Orthodox bishops, which counted for a great deal even in the time of Clovis, and for incalculably more in the next two or three centuries. Meanwhile it is evident that the conversion of the Franks brought even a greater gain to the Roman and Gallic Orthodox Churches than it brought to Clovis and his subjects.

A recent historian has said that "the motives which induced Clovis to accept baptism and to profess faith in the Crucified One were of the meanest, poorest, and most unspiritual kind. Few men have been further from that which Christ called 'the Kingdom of Heaven' than this grasping and brutal Prankish chief, to whom robbery, falsehood, murder were, after his baptism as much as before it (perhaps even more than before it), the ordinary steps in the ladder of his elevation."

There is much truth in the remark; but the measure of the truth is only to be estimated when we have decided upon the true historical scale of measurement. It would be idle to compare Clovis, as a man of arms, with anything higher than the typical fighting Frank of his age and race, or, as a Christian, with anything more fit for the Kingdom of Heaven than the Burgundian bishop who wrote to him, on the morrow of his conversion: "So often as you fight, we conquer." To fight was his virtue; to grasp fresh territory was his noble ambition; to rob and to slay were his ancestral mode and tradition of warfare. A greater crime than all these was false-hood and treachery. We shall see that Clovis is accused of both these things by a man who was almost his contemporary, and who had every reason to take a lenient view of his conduct.

In any case it is clear that Clovis did not suffer by his repudiation of the Teutonic deities, and he was quite entitled to think that the God of the Christians gave help to true believers. The channels through which that aid reached him were Clotilda, the Orthodox bishops, and the Councils which they were constantly holding throughout the country, wherever there was a trouble to allay, or a quarrel to compose, or an incipient mutiny against the authority of the Church to overawe. The bishops could raise wars, secure allies, and restore peace; the clergy could check popular and servile discontents, look after the sick and the poor, make the women more gentle and serviceable, conciliate the Gauls and the Romans, and even facilitate the collection of the taxes. Certainly Clovis had ample cause for satisfaction. All he had to do was to fight as his father fought, to add victory to victory and kingdom to kingdom, and to do honour to the God of Clotilda.

Chapter VI

The Subjection of Gaul

Clovis offered terms to the Armorican cities in 497. The cities accepted these terms, and recognized the rule of the Franks, just ninety years after they had declared themselves free of the Roman military and civil authority. Yet it is doubtful whether they would have accepted the new authority, however easy the conditions, if it had not been for the good offices of their bishops.

Whose was the master mind at this crisis amongst the Orthodox bishops of the Western Church, whether Remigius, or Avitus of Vienne, or Gelasius of Rome, or Anastasius who succeeded Gelasius, and wrote a letter of congratulation to welcome Clovis into the fold, is not quite clear. Nor is it clear whether the bishops suggested to Clovis, or he suggested to them, that Arian heretics like the kings of the Burgundians and the Visigoths could not be allowed to establish themselves permanently between the sacred city of Rome and the champion whom God had raised up for her in the north. Such ideas must have occurred simultaneously to the bishops and to Clovis, for they were in the natural line of development of the ambitions of both.

But it is not likely that either side would think of hurrying forward on a career of conquest in advance of suitable occasion and pretext. About 495 Theodoric, king of the Ostrogoths, who ruled at Ravenna and held sway over Rome, had married Augofleda, the elder sister of Clovis. Ostrogoths and Visigoths continued to live on terms of mutual amity, and it would have been perilous, as well as impolitic, to precipitate a quarrel with either of these nations. But Theodoric himself was not well disposed to the Burgundians, and it was understood beforehand that war was inevitable between Clovis and the uncle of Clotilda.

Gundobald had murdered the father and mother of Clotilda. His brother Godegisil, bearing this in mind, and thinking it wise to make terms for himself with Clovis at the expense of Gundobald, sent a secret messenger to the king of the Franks, offering to be his man. "If you will help me," he frankly said, "against my brother the king, so that I may either kill him or drive him out of the country, I will pay you every year such tribute as you may decide upon." Here, then, was the pretext or occasion for which Clovis had waited; and, in the last year of the fifth century, he prepared an expedition, and led his army southwards.

Then Gundobald sent to Godegisil and said :

"Come and help me, for the Franks are moving, and they have made up their minds to seize our lands. Let us therefore be as one against our enemies, lest they should make us suffer what others have suffered." For Gundobald and Godegisil were already at rivalry; but Gundobald did not know that his brother had written to the Frank. And Godegisil answered, "I will bring an army and help you."

So Godegisil came to his brother ; and the army of the Franks, which had waited for the arrival of the traitor, came into touch with the Burgundians, and there was a great battle. And Godegisil suddenly turned round upon his brother, and Gundobald saw that he had been betrayed. He fought bravely for a long time, but his army was cut to pieces, and he himself escaped with difficulty to Avenio, which we call Avignon. Then Godegisil triumphed as if he had been the conqueror; but Clovis followed Gundobald to the valley of the Durance, for he saw that he was too brave an enemy to leave behind him.

Now Gundobald had a friend in Avenio, by name Aredius, who seems to have been a Gallo-Roman, and was certainly a witty and resourceful man. And the king opened his heart to Aredius, and said : "Valiant me undique angustiae, et quid faciam ignoro" — "My enemies close me in on every side, and there is no way out of my difficulties." Aredius listened to him, and bade him not despair, " for I," said he, "will go to the king of the Franks, and will take care that he shall destroy neither you nor your country. Only promise to do what is necessary in your own interest". And Gundobald promised.

Then Aredius went to Clovis, and said he had come from the luckless Gundobald, and wished to devote himself for ever to the service of the conqueror.

The Frank eagerly welcomed his new adherent — for he was just the kind of adherent that a Teutonic king always welcomed, and perhaps rarely secured, amongst the Roman inhabitants of the conquered lands. Aredius was "jocundus in fabulis, strenuus in consiliis, Justus in judiciis, et in commisso fidelis ;" and, when he had made his impression as a good companion and a teller of capital stories, he ventured one day to give the fierce barbarian a little common-sense advice. "This Gundobald," he said, "is shut up in the town, which is very strong. You are not making much headway against him, but your army is eating up the crops, and destroying the vines and olives. Why not impose a tribute on him, and leave this rich country to supply part of the money which must come into your hands?" The Teuton king was persuaded — as nearly every Teutonic leader could be persuaded by a plausible Roman. He sent to Gundobald to demand ransom, and a yearly tribute, which the Burgundian readily promised; and Clovis withdrew his army from the Rhone country. But Gundobald did not keep his promises; and perhaps Aredius was specially careful, after that, not to fall again into the hands of Clovis.

Gundobald recovered his army and his kingdom, and hunted down his brother Godegisil at Vienne, and put him to death. Then we are told that he "established a milder code of laws for the Burgundians, so as to prevent their Magistrates from dealing harshly with the Romans." This is the Burgundian code known as the *Lex Gondoboda*, or *Loi Gombette* — one of the famous barbarian Codes which go far to prove, as indeed we already know from Tacitus, that the name of barbarian must not be too indiscriminately applied to the Teutonic races.

If the records of the time were not so disappointingly thin, we should be able to reconstruct the situation as it now stood with far more confidence and precision. But the few writers who deal as contemporaries with the events under consideration paid no attention to dates, and did not attempt to make their narrative reasonably continuous. One is almost tempted to think that a man like Gregory of Tours, who clearly had something of the instinct of a historian (though without any historic style), must have had more method in his work than is apparent in his "History of the Franks," and that he or someone else cut out many passages from the account as he originally wrote it. It is easy to understand that he would think it no part of his duty to report all the consultations and conclusions of the Orthodox bishops in regard to their policy towards the Arians, or to their manipulation or direction of Clovis. But he rarely mentions the national or provincial Councils of the Gallic Church, at which the relations of the Church and the States were doubtless (more or less formally and openly) brought under discussion, although these Councils were held every few years, and sometimes year after year. It is not by any means improbable, it may rather be looked upon as a matter of course, that the Gallic bishops, in their keen anxiety to deliver the country from heresy, and to make the most of their new instrument for this purpose, gave the Arians ample cause to think that a crisis was approaching, and that a deliberate attempt would be made to deprive them of the freedom of belief and worship which they had secured under the Gothic and Burgundian kings.

It so happens that we have no record of a Council in Gaul between that of Aries in 475 and that of Lyon in 500. The explanation may be that the peacemakers were for a time in the ascendant, and that negotiations were being patiently carried on with the object of bringing about an agreement between the Orthodox and Arian bishops. At any rate, the two parties met in council at Lyon in the last year of the century, four years after the conversion of Clovis ; and it may even be that the summoning of this council of conciliation led Clovis to put a lame conclusion to his war with Gundobald, and thus to lose the political fruits of his victory. If the Burgundian war had come after the failure of the Council — for it did fail — it is most unlikely that Clovis would have suffered Gundobald to ride off with a promise, and Burgundy to slip out of his hands.

Conciliation had failed. The Arian States knew that the Orthodox bishops would never meet them on the point of doctrine, and would never rest so long as there was a chance of weakening or destroying them. They were nervous, for a twofold reason, about the growing power of Clovis; but against Clovis they were able to set the strong man of the south, who from Ravenna overawed both the feeble emperor at Constantinople and the feeble authorities at Rome. Moreover, they had the tactical advantage of occupying an unbroken zone of Arian power and influence, extending from the Danube to the western sea, and from the Mediterranean to the

Loire, between the Orthodox ecclesiastics in the south and the Orthodox Franks in the north. It was, indeed, a formidable confederation, and it speaks much for the awe which Clovis had recently inspired that even Theodoric, the master of Italy, half of Gaul, and a large part of Spain, could not feel any confidence in the issue without making special efforts to detach the Eastern and Central Franks from the headstrong convert of Reims.

The first five years of the sixth century were consumed in preparations, deliberations, and patient watching for opportunity — Clovis in the meanwhile striking another blow at the restless Allemans. The strategy of the Arians, seeing that they undoubtedly expected an attack from Clovis, is not what one would have looked for in Theodoric and his allies. Alaric had assembled his army in the north-western corner of Aquitaine, away from his capital, and as far as possible from his father-in-law, on whom he relied for assistance in case of need. It is true that he did his best to gain time, and to avoid giving Clovis the pretext for which he seemed to be waiting. He even asked Clovis for a friendly interview, which took place — the time, more important than the place, is not mentioned — on an island in the Loire, near to the modern Amboise. There they ate and drank together, and vowed friendship, and parted, as Gregory says, "pacifici."

In 506 two things happened in the south of Aquitaine, at places not very many miles asunder, which stood to each other almost certainly in the relation of cause and effect. Quintian, bishop of the Ruteni, living in the town which is now called Rodez, fell into disfavour with the citizens because he was ready, or because they thought he was ready, to welcome the rule of the Franks. He being Orthodox, whilst the majority of the citizens would probably be Arians, such a suspicion might easily occur during the excitement caused by an immediate expectation of war. Alaric was at this time with his army at Poitiers. The affair at Rodez came to an open dispute, and Quintian was privately warned that there was a plot against his life. So he escaped with a few priests, and betook himself to the neighbouring territory of the Arvernians, where he was welcomed by Bishop Eufrasius, who gave him "houses and fields and vineyards," saying that the Church of the Arvernians was quite rich enough to support two bishops. Now, it was in the same year 506 that a council of the Orthodox Church was held at Agde, a coast-town on the other side of the Cevennes ; and, whether the Council was held before or after the disturbance at Rodez, it does not seem to be a violent supposition to conclude that there was a connection of some sort between the two events. The significance, in that case, would be much the same, whether the Council met at Agde because of the troubles that had arisen in Rodez, or whether the Arians at Rodez were excited by reports brought from Agde, where Quintian would in all likelihood have attended the gathering of the clergy. If the Council, which met on September 11th, came after the ill-treatment of Quintian, there would be much exasperation amongst the Orthodox Christians; and the incident would not be without effect on the proceedings of Clovis.

"And so," Gregory abruptly says at this point, "Clovis the king said to his *leudes*; 'it goes very much against the grain with me that these Arians should hold any part of Gaul. Let us go forth with the help of the Lord, and overthrow them, and make their land our own'" The summons was greeted with joy, and preparations were made for an advance.

In the spring of 507 Clovis led out his army, and marched through the country round about Tours, on the way to Poitiers. The character of the compact between Clovis and the Church was rendered very manifest in this campaign. The king issued strict orders that his army was to touch nothing whatever, except grass for the horses, during its progress through the country which had been governed by the holy Bishop Martin. The Teutonic warrior was on his way to champion the cause of orthodoxy, and miraculous appearances were vouchsafed to him, so that he and his men were convinced that they were under the special protection of Heaven. Bearing in mind his experience in the battle of Tolbiac, Clovis pledged himself to a pious recognition of the Divine favour if victory should be vouchsafed to him ; and thus it was an army with the spirit of crusaders which finally came in sight of Alaric, in the Vocladensian Plain (near the modern Vouglé). The Goths were the first to attack, and the battle was obstinately fought; but it ended in the rout of the Arian host, and the slaughter of Alaric by his ruthless enemy. Clovis had a narrow escape from death at the hands of two Gothic lancers, but the speed of his horse or the strength of his mail sufficed to save him.

Pushing southward without delay, he took the rich seaport of Burdigala (Bordeaux), which was one of the chief centres of academic learning as well as of trade in Gaul, and, marching along the right bank of the Garumna, secured Tolosa, the capital of the Visigoth kingdom. In the following year he besieged Carcaso (Carcassonne), between Toulouse and Narbonne.

The dominion of the Visigoths in Aquitaine, excluding the Pyrenean and maritime provinces, was now practically wiped out. Less than a hundred years had passed since Atolph, brother-in-law of the earlier and greater Alaric, had made his first entry in the Narbonensian province, and barely ninety since Tolosa became the capital of Visigothic Gaul. The Visigoths left but faint traces of their occupation; yet here again we have to make a significant exception in regard to the codification of the law. Apparently one of the last acts of Alaric II was to nominate a commission of bishops and Roman jurisconsults, who were charged to summarise the principles and practice of Roman law. They based their labours to a large extent on the code of Theodosius, published in 438, which reduced into a comprehensive summary the *Jus privatum* the law of administration and government, the criminal law, the fiscal laws, the laws of procedure and local administration, and the ecclesiastical law. Some modification of these maxims was introduced by the Visigothic commission, mainly for the purpose of alleviating their severity and strengthening the principle of impartiality. The "Breviarium" of Anianus, as it was called, after the name of the president of the commission, survived in the courts of Gaul and Spain for several centuries.

The conquests of Clovis in the south were now checked by the Ostrogothic king. Theodoric, as we have said, had been anxious to prevent the war between Clovis and Alaric, even to the extent of appealing to the other Teutonic and Arian nations to take common action for the preservation of the Visigothic kingdom. The rapidity of the movements of Clovis in 506 had anticipated anything that could have been done in this sense; but, even apart from that, it was not likely that the Eastern or Riparian Franks would conspire against the ruler of Tournai and Soissons in order to play the game of the Goths in Italy and Gaul. Another reason which accounts for the failure of Theodoric's earlier plan is that Gundobald the Burgundian, whose interest was certainly to propitiate Clovis rather than to give him further cause of offence, was now in league with the Franks; whilst Theodoric himself was much absorbed in his quarrel with Anastasius, which made it difficult for him to quit Ravenna for Gaul, or even to dispatch an army to the assistance of his son-in-law. So much, however, he did contrive to do, sending his general Ibbas to oppose the Franks under his namesake Theodoric, the eldest son of Clovis. The combined forces of Theodoric and Gundobald were gradually reducing the whole of Southern Aquitaine, when at last the intervention of the Ostrogoths became effectual, and the Franks and Burgundians, in the absence of Clovis, were defeated by Ibbas. The greater part of the Narbonensian province, east of the Cevennes, was restored to Amalaric, the son of Alaric, whilst the older Roman province of Gaul was added to the dominion of the Ostrogoths. It was not long before the mutual enmities of these three kings, Clovis, Theodoric, and Gundobald, were patched up by a common understanding. Clovis was confirmed in the possession of his conquests down to the borders of Gascony and Septimania, including the city of Toulouse ; and east.

Meanwhile he appears under a new and extraordinary guise, as a Consul if not as an Augustus of the Roman Empire. The titles, or at any rate that of consul, were conferred upon him by the aged Emperor Anastasius, in recognition of his victory over the Visigoths; for Anastasius, involved as he himself was in the Monophysite controversy, seems none the less to have been moved to show honour to the champion of the Trinitarian principle against the Arian heretics, who was at the same time at enmity with the masterful ruler of the Ostrogoths. Clovis evidently took huge delight in his new dignities, his Roman robes and his somewhat farcical diadem. The fierce barbarian rejoiced with childish glee in the toys which the emperor had sent him, and his courtiers were ready to fall in with his humour by addressing him as consul or pro-consul. Many of the ancient forms and traditions of Rome were kept alive at Constantinople with punctilious exactitude, and it may be that the consular rank was bestowed on Clovis by virtue of his temporary possession of the old maritime province of Cisalpine Gaul.

It was apparently at this time that Clovis, brought nearer to Roman ideas by his conversion, by twelve years of association with the Orthodox clergy, and now by his consulship, bethought himself how Julian, Valentinian, and Gratian had dwelt at Lutetia on the Seine. Thither, at any rate, he moved his family and his court; but Paris was not yet destined to become the capital even of Western Francia. Clovis lived and died there; and though he had begun his reign as a Frank of the Franks, and a determined enemy of Rome, he now delighted in the imitation of Roman customs, dressing in purple robes, writing to his brother-in-law to send him a *citharaedus* in order that he might have music at his banquets, and appointing his commission of learned men to revise the Latin version of the old Salic Law. Was it in any sense on a Roman pattern that he modeled his dealings with his brother Franks during the last few years of his life? He had no sooner become a dignitary of the Roman Empire than he prepared to strike down his actual or possible rivals for the supremacy of the Franks.

It is no part of the duty of one who relates a story from historical sources either to defend the character of his actors or to moralize over their evil deeds. At the same time, it is not enough to repeat in bald terms the bare statements even of contemporary writers. The historian who writes long after the transaction of a particular group or series of events is often better qualified than a contemporary to estimate the significance of facts and the character of individuals; just as it is easier to observe and describe the proportions of a building from the outside than from the inside, or the characteristics of a landscape from a distance than from the midst of it.

What is necessary is that we should regard the central figures of history, not merely as man-slayers, or as founders or destroyers of states, but as creatures of their time helping to create the times which succeed them, and as instruments working to certain ends under certain conditions. Neither aspect should be left out of sight; but it is unquestionably more important to place a character accurately amidst its historical surroundings than to discuss its goodness or badness in comparison with men and women of the present day.

Clovis was fierce, formidable, and generally unrelenting, but he carried out, with no greater cruelty than that of civilized Roman conquerors, the ambitions cherished by his Teutonic ancestors for four or five centuries. He availed himself of the treachery of Godegisil, but he was easily persuaded to spare Gundobald. He accepted Christianity with mixed motives, but certainly under the influence of a pure and loving wife. He was ruthless in the slaughter of Alaric; but Alaric, since his pledge of friendship, had failed to protect the Orthodox bishops in Aquitaine, had assumed the offensive, and called in the aid of Theodoric. We know that the enemies of Clovis hated him, whilst his neighbours suspected and feared him; but all that we hear of him as a brother, a husband, and a father, is without exception good.

Full of faults as Clovis may have been, violent, gusty, unscrupulous in pursuing his larger ambitions, we are scarcely prepared by what has gone before for the record of his last two years. This is what Gregory of Tours has to say about it : — Whilst Clovis was resting at Paris he privately sent word to Cloderic, son of Siegbert the Lame, who had fought on his side at Vouglé — as Siegbert had fought with him against the Allemans — suggesting to him that his father had grown old and decrepit, and that if he should happen to die the wealth which had been accumulated by Siegbert, as well as the kingdom of the Rhinelands, would in the ordinary course fall into the hands of Cloderic. So much as this, no doubt, Clovis might have said, without any sinister purpose, in answer to a question as to his own wishes and intentions concerning the succession. But Gregory takes the darker view, saying that Clovis sent his message secretly in order to stimulate Cloderic to action.

However this may be, Cloderic resolved to be king without further delay. One day Siegbert rode out of Cologne and crossed the Rhine, intending to spend the afternoon in the "Burconian" wood — that is, the wood of Duisburg, about two miles from the right bank of the river. As the midday heat came on, he rested beneath an awning, and, whilst he slept, the assassins hired by his son came in and slew him.

Cloderic then sent word to Clovis, saying, "My father is dead, and his treasures are mine. Send trusty men, to whom I may give whatever you desire." And Clovis sent messengers, who asked Cloderic to show them the treasure; and, whilst the murderer was stooping over a chest of gold, they stabbed him in the back. When Clovis knew that the son had paid the penalty of his crime he came to Cologne, and addressed the *leudes* denying his responsibility for the two murders, and suggesting that the Franks of the Rhinelands should accept his protection. The proposal was received with acclamation, and he was forthwith raised upon a shield and saluted as king.

Now came the turn of Cararic, who ruled over the Northern Franks between Teruenna and the sea. Clovis accused Cararic of holding back in the war against Syagrius, and of playing him false in his struggle against the Gallo- Romans. Having secured the persons of the king and his son, he degraded them in the old Frank fashion, on which he had improved after embracing Christianity, by shaving their heads and devoting them to the religious life, in token that their days of warriorship were ended. The son consoled his father by saying that their hair would grow again, and that they would be avenged; but the words were reported to Clovis, who ordered his captives to be slain, and added their kingdom to his own dominions.

Ragnacar, the king at Cambrai was the next victim. In this case the task of Clovis was all the easier because the vices of Ragnacar and one of his favourites had excited the disgust of his subjects, who made little or no resistance to the invader, but delivered their king into his hands. Ragnacar was led bound into the presence of Clovis, who, feigning indignation, demanded of his prisoner, "Why have you disgraced our race by suffering yourself to be bound? It would have been better for you to die." And, suiting the action to the word, he smote Ragnacar on the head with his axe, and slew him. Then, all his relatives having been removed, he publicly lamented, as Gregory tells us, that he was "left as a stranger amongst strange people, without a kinsman to stand by him if misfortune should befall him." Either the bishop, or the bishop's corrupted text, with an utter absence of consistency, suggests that Clovis was only seeking to ascertain if any of the Franks would claim to be a member of his family, so that his work of extermination might be complete; though in connection with the same events we are assured that every day God cast down his enemies, and added increase to his kingdom, because he walked before Him with an upright heart, and did what was pleasing in His eyes.

Soon after these events Clovis died at Paris, and was buried in the church of the Holy Apostles, which he and the Queen Clotilda had combined to build. He passed away, says Gregory, in the fifth year after the battle with Alaric; and the days of his reign were thirty years, and the span of his life was forty-five years. Queen Clotilda, after the death of her husband, came to live at Tours, and there she abode all the days of her life, rarely visiting Paris, but rendering Christian service at the basilica of St Martin, with all modesty and benevolence.

Chapter VII
Characteristics of the Franks

Though we may not yet speak of France as a kingdom created by the Franks in Gaul, at any rate we have the Franks exercising dominion in the land from which they were never to be expelled, and which they never wholly abandoned. Their laws, their customs, their characteristics, were now planted in Gallic soil, and bore fruit, not only from the original sap, but also in some sense from the sap of the stocks on which they were grafted. Kelts, Teutons of the pre-historic settlements — whom we have included under the name of Gauls — Romans, Gallo-Romans, Britons, Gascons, even Goths and Burgundians, were all concerned with the Franks in compounding the nation to which the last-mentioned people gave their name, but not their language, and to which all contributed in varying proportion their physical, domestic, and intellectual qualities. Let us take a rapid survey of some of the more conspicuous national characteristics of the Franks.

The confederated tribes whose border-wars with Rome had welded them into a distinct people, and prepared them for definite nationalization, cannot in the truest sense be said to have assumed a national type until they were both settled as regards territory and governed by the administration of a settled law.

So far as settled territory is concerned, we have seen that Franks had been established in Brabant from before the time of Julian, more than a hundred years before the occupation of what was afterwards called Flanders, Artois, and Northern Picardy. These earlier Frank settlers, it is true, were bound to Rome by an obligation of military service, an obligation which they doubtless discharged so long as Rome was powerful enough to enforce it. But at any rate they were settled; the institutions of a settled people had time to strike root, and the laws of their ancestors were brought together, written down, and consistently applied in the administration of justice. Then, at length, there would be a community of interests under a single impersonal authority, which would deserve to be called a nation.

At what time this bringing together of the Frank laws in a written code took place, it would be impossible to say. The Salic Law, such as we find it in the most ancient Latin translations, is specially attributed, in one of the titles, to the nation of the Franks living between the Carbonarian forest (partly corresponding with the Ardennes) and the river Ligeris (Lys). Some take Ligeris here to mean the Loire. But there was never a time at which the recognized possessions of the Franks could be described as lying between the Ardennes and the Loire.

The description is just conceivable as applied to the dominion of Clovis alone, immediately before and after his marriage — which, to be sure, was not an unlikely time for the translation of the ancient code into Latin. But elsewhere the text speaks of the Franks as being governed "per proceres." This expression may have been left standing by the carelessness of the translator. The date of the translation, however, is not a question which lends itself to confident statement.

Now the country between the Ardennes and the river Lys is the district which may be regarded as the third zone of Frank settlement — Batavia being the first, Brabant the second, Hainault the third, and Flanders the fourth; and the time of settlement was, roughly speaking, between the concessions of Julian to the Salians in 358 and the invasion of Clodion in 447. All these settlers would, as a matter of course, have their own customs and laws, if not identical yet closely similar for all the Franks and their most neighbourly allies. In intervals of peace the chiefs and their *leudes* the men of religion and counsel, would meet together, to administer, or build upon, or, if necessary, collect, the laws of their ancestors.

The fact of our finding the earliest copy of the Salic code with a defined application to the third zone of settlement does not, of course, in any way prove that the code originated with the Franks of Hainault, or that the Salic law was in a special sense the law of the Belgian Salians. The code comes down to us as that which was in force under the Merovingian dynasty, and the identity of the laws observed in Hainault with the laws promulgated by Clovis is enough in itself to show that they were the common laws of the Western Salian Franks, extending from the Scheidungenburg, on the borders of Thuringia, to the mouths of the Rhine, Scheldt, and Somme, and afterwards over a great part of Gaul.

It is fair to conclude that, early in the fifth century, there was a Salic, or Salian, code wherever there was a strong Salian chief ruling over a defined territory, and that all these codes were fundamentally one and the same. In any case the laws of the Franks, as of other Germans, existed in their own tongue before they were translated into Latin for the benefit of the Gallo-Romans, and of the Latin clerics who would naturally assist in expounding them. Grimm, indeed, was of opinion that the Salic law itself came into existence in the fifth century, being composed in Latin by jurists who would necessarily use many indigenous words in a Latinised form. But, as Mr. Hessels points out, all the material for such a composition would be in existence beforehand, so that the work of these jurists, whilst it probably amounted to a codification, must also have been in the nature of a translation, article by article, and perhaps phrase by phrase. "Due allowance being made for the legendary character" of statements concerning the origin of the code, "we may fairly infer from the Prologues that, in the tradition of the Franks, their Salic Law dated from a period considerably anterior to the fifth century, and had remained essentially the same, notwithstanding such modifications and additions as became necessary in course of time." A Latin version before the acceptance of Christianity by the Franks need not create much surprise or difficulty for those who consider that war had not been the only mode of interchange between the Roman and the Teuton. There had been a traffic of thought and culture, as well as of merchandise, even across the Lower Rhine ; and amongst the Franks there would certainly be many who understood the Latin tongue, and some who had consulted the law of Rome. There had been Roman captives and settlers in Germany, as well as German captives and settlers in Gaul; thousands of German mercenaries in the Roman army must have returned to their native land after acquiring a

Roman tongue; and many generations of trade and intermarriage must have contributed to a set of conditions which made a Latin version of the law a thing to be desired.

It will be interesting to glance at some of the more characteristic features of the Teutonic law prior to the year 500, and of the national customs and institutions from which their written laws had been evolved.

The most characteristic features in any body of law will be found in its method of dealing with offences committed by individuals against the interests of the community, resolving itself into various forms of vindication or punishment, and into a system of alternatives allowed by the community for the avoidance of punishment. Such alternatives to punishment are the first signs of mitigation in the law, based as it naturally is, in the first instance, on the cruelties of total or partial suppression. Now the root-fact of Teutonic law in this secondary phase of mitigation was the institution of *wehrgeld* or money paid in redemption of crime. And a further characteristic of Teutonic law was its clear conception of the double character of crime. Wherever there was an offence against an individual, it was recognized that there was also an offence against the community; and the administrators of the law were not content — as was generally the case amongst the Romans — to punish on behalf of the community without regard to the damage suffered by the individual. In fact, the vindication of the individual (when crime touched an individual) was always the most prominent idea of Teutonic punishments. The redress of the injured person under the authority of law was a substitution for the natural right of private vengeance; and the Teuton saw that the vindication of individuals was a vindication and a defense for the State. This simple intuition gave a distinct character to Teutonic law, which has counted for much in the national developments of the Teutonic race. There was amongst the Teutons a systematic scale of *wehrgeld*, based not only upon the nature of the crime, but also upon the status of the injured person; and the system itself introduced a further mitigation by the fact that individual sufferers had a stronger motive than the State for accepting a pecuniary indemnity for a wrong inflicted upon them. In most cases the offender had to pay a fine to the royal treasury (known by the name of "fredum," or peace-making), as well as to indemnify his victim. When the parties concerned were slow in coming to an agreement, the judge intervened to hasten the settlement; and he also had the power, in circumstances of special aggravation, to double or treble the stipulated payment.

Wehrgeld differed, as above said, according to the status of the injured person. Amongst the Franks, the highest class after the king was that of the king's *leudes* and nobles, the latter, under the Merovingians (and before their time) being *criniti*, or families entitled or accustomed to wear their hair long ; and after them came the *antrustions*. Of the Leti, or Lites, settled on the land, we have spoken elsewhere.

Below them were the slaves, and amongst the slaves there was a varying estimation of value, decided according to their worth in the eyes of their masters. The payment of wehrgeld did not, at any rate in the earlier periods, apply to offences against the king, or to public crimes.

Another institution of the Teutons arising out of the commission of crime was that of the urtkeil, or ordeal, which was the judgment or detection of the criminal by means of an appeal to the deity, which was naturally resorted to in the absence of personal witnesses. It was, in this older and less superstitious sense, a sort of sacrament and act of faith, employed with all sincerity in the belief that God would judge between the wrongdoer and his victim when human means failed to provide a remedy. The Church not only sanctioned this form of ordeal, but also added to its solemnity by requiring that the parties concerned — that is to say, the victim and the person suspected of the crime — should attend mass and communicate. Then, in the case of ordeal by boiling water, which is mentioned in the Salic Law, the priest blessed the water, and a ring or a stone, suspended by a cord, was immersed, three times in succession, at increasing depths. The person called upon to undergo the ordeal had to draw out the ring or stone, and his arm was afterwards wrapped in bandages for three days. If, at the end of that time, his flesh had not recovered its ordinary appearance, his guilt was held to be proved.

Ordeal by cold water, which survived for many centuries as a test of witchcraft, required that the arm of the suspected person should be bound to his leg, and that he should be thrown into a pond, his guilt being declared if he floated instead of sinking.

The ordeal of the cross was, in effect, a trial of endurance between two suspected or mutually accused persons, who had to stand with extended arms whilst divine service was proceeding; and the one who first dropped his arms stood convicted.

Ordeal by hot iron consisted in holding a heated bar in the hand, or walking barefoot over hot iron bars or plates.

In ordeal by fire, the person submitted to the test had to walk, with the consecrated host in his hands, between two adjacent fires.

Another form of decision in contested cases was to employ the Gospels after the manner of the *sortes Virgilianœ*, The book was opened, and an oracle was drawn from the first sentence of the page exposed.

Ordeal by single combat involved the loss of a hand by the defeated combatant; or, in the most serious cases, he was buried alive. This, and the ordeal by cold water, survived longer than the other forms. Charles the Great forbade the ordeal of the cross as tending to profanity.

The law affecting slavery amongst the Franks — concerning which something will be found hereafter, in the fifteenth chapter of the present work — again contrasts favourably with the severity of Roman institutions. The manumission of slaves, which, especially after the adoption of Christianity, was a frequent operation in an epoch and in a country which knew more than one or two modes of reduction to the state of slavery, was effected in various ways, described in the Formulas preserved for us by Marculfus, a monk of Frank origin, who wrote in the seventh century, and therefore dealt in particular with the Merovingian age. Enfranchisement per denarium was the most formal and symbolic of these methods. When a master was prepared to liberate his slave, he took him before the count of his district, to whom he announced his intention.

Thereupon the slave produced a coin, and offered it to his master as a sign that he wished to purchase his freedom. The master, not receiving the denarius, but striking it from the hand of his slave, signified that he was willing to complete the contract, and at the same time to forgo the price. A *carta denarialis* was then drawn up by the order of the count, and delivered to the former slave as evidence of his emancipation; and the latter (as indicated in the Riparian law) assumed or resumed the condition of a free-born man.

Another mode of enfranchisement (traced back to the Chamavians) was per *handtradam* when the slave was surrounded by a ring of twelve persons, one of whom was his master, and this master took the slave and passed him outside the circle — a written charter being subsequently given, as in the case previously described.

Yet another mode of enfranchisement amongst the Franks was by the master's last will and testament, when, as Marculfus says, the owner liberated all his slaves "for the remission of his sins and the salvation of his soul." But this case of emancipation was regarded as inferior in kind to the other two, for it did not confer the complete civil rights acquired by those who had earned their freedom before their masters came within sight of death.

Chapter VII

The Mayors of the Palace

From the beginning of the seventh century the history of the Franks includes more and more frequent mention of certain honourable and influential persons associated in the government of the country, to whom it is now necessary that we should devote special attention. These are the Mayors of the Palace.

The Major Domus, or *Magister Palatii*, was a functionary appointed during the last century and a half of the Merovingian dynasty to exercise authority in the palace and household of the king. The term itself was borrowed from the old imperial regime. The office, under the Franks, was the creation of circumstances; the officer, who would be able to relieve a strong king of some of the more irksome of his duties, would be indispensable when the king was fighting at a distance from his principal palaces, or when he was a minor. It would be necessary that his authority and his administrative power should extend over the *leudes*; and thus he would inevitably be, from the beginning, the most important man in the kingdom, after the king. It cannot be said with certainty who was the first Frank Mayor of the Palace, or under what circumstances he was appointed.

The office doubtless existed before the Latin name : the most influential of the king's *leudes* may have discharged such functions as those just mentioned soon after the house of Merowig was established at Soissons, or, at any rate, soon after Clovis extended his kingdom to the western sea. Whether the Mayor increased in authority step by step from small beginnings, or — as is more likely — was established by the *leudes* as a check on the abuse of power by the king and his family, at all events we first hear of him at a time when some check of this kind was absolutely necessary.

It seems probable that the simultaneous presence of the two queen-mothers, Brunhilda and Fredegonda, in the two palaces of Metz and Tournai, and the extraordinary part which they played in the affairs of the Franks, did more than anything else to call the office into existence, or to give it its special importance. Certain it is that the strong line of Mayors of the Palace in the seventh and eighth centuries led ultimately to the downfall of the Merovingian dynasty. Both Fredegonda and Brunhilda had been seriously embroiled with the *leudes* of their sons or grandsons. The Franks were well accustomed to the counsels and even to the strictures of their women; but, as the Salic law excluded women from succession to estates, so the fighting men and the court officers, the judges, administrators, and clergy, would be sure to watch with jealousy, and seriously to resent, the endless intrigues and disastrous machinations of the queens. Fredegonda was more than once in danger from the leudes at Toumai. Brunhilda's quarrel with the *leudes* at Metz came to a crisis, as we have seen, by her compassing the death of Duke Wintrion of Champagne, and being driven out of the country in the following year (599).

During the minority of Childebert, about the year 575, the Major Domus was in no sense the king's creature and instrument, or his appointed representative with the *leudes*; he became rather the representative of the aristocracy at the court, and the overseer of the king. In this change the power of the aristocracy was making itself felt, though the innovation was strenuously resisted by a monarch here and there, and doggedly opposed by the queen Brunhilda, until her party was defeated, and she herself was captured by Clotair. Clotair, as we have seen, united the Frank kingdoms under his sway, but even he was forced by the Austrian and Burgundian aristocracies to promise that he would not interfere in the elections of the Mayors of the Palace. He swore, moreover, to Warnaher, Mayor of Burgundy, and Rade of Austria, not to dispossess them of their offices. According to a chronicler, Clotair was a "patient" monarch, and he seems to have played his cards with considerable success. On the death of Warnaher, in 626, he asked the Burgundians if they would elect a new Mayor. This invitation, as Clotair had doubtless anticipated, they declined, asking that they might be allowed to treat separately with the king. The return to the old system, however, brought about a State of aggravated anarchy and disunion much more serious than the internal dissensions which existed at the same time in Austria, where the continuance of the mayoralty formed a kind of national balance of powers.

Clotair II died in 628, and was succeeded by his son Dagobert.

Dagobert contrived to keep his brother Charibert out of his inheritance, and in 630 was in full enjoyment of authority. But the aristocracy was distinctly against him, though the prudence of Pepin of Landen, the Mayor of Austria, restrained them from openly breaking with the king. At length, under pressure of an invasion of the Slavonians (633), Dagobert agreed to recognize a separate government for Austria, and he nominated as king his three-yeftr-old son, Siegbert II., with Grimoald, son of Pepin, and Otho to manage the kingdom, while Pepin was to live in Neustria.

Dagobert was one of the most kingly monarchs of the Merovingian line, and the little that we are told of him creates the desire to know considerably more. He revised and promulgated the laws of the Franks, and was a patron of the ecclesiastical schokirs and artists of his day. He fought many battles, most of them successfully, headed an expedition into Spain, suppressed a revolt of the Gascons, and broke the growing power of the kings of Brittany. Amongst his ministers were S. Audoenus (Ouen), his chancellor, and S. Eligius (Eloi), his "magister nummorum," a famous worker in gold, who designed and adorned many thrones (including that of Dagobert), tombs (including that of S. Germain, bishop of Paris), and other details of church and palace architecture, with the taste of a true artist. Though he had never been ordained, Eligius was made bishop of Noyon; he founded several abbeys, and was long held in peculiar reverence. To swear by Saint Eloy, as Chaucer tells us, was held a venial oath for nuns and friars. He seems to have been an artist in words as well as in gold, and left behind him a number of popular homilies. His life was written by his friend St. Ouen, and is preserved for us in the "Spicilegium" of the Benedictine bookworm Achéry.

Dagobert's death in 638 marked the beginning of a series of Merovingian *rois faineants* lasting for about a century. Dagobert himself had shown something of the earlier Merovingian force in an attempt to impose Christianity upon the Frisians, and he founded the first Christian church at Utrecht Ega, who had been appointed by Dagobert guardian of his infant son Clovis, now became Mayor of Neustria, whilst Pepin returned to Metz. In the following year Grimoald, on the death of his father, secured the position of sole Major Domus of Austria, though only after considerable trouble from Otho, described as the "bajulus" of Siegbert, who was slain in 642 by a partisan of Grimoald's. Some years later Grimoald caused Dagobert, son of Siegbert, to be shorn and sent to Ireland, while he set his own child, Childebert, on the throne. The mass of the people, however, refused to recognize this act, and finally both father and son were slain. Grimoald met the fate of many prescient persons who are too eager to assist the natural course of evolution. He had anticipated coming events by something like a century.

The table on the opposite page (which should be compared with that at the end of the twelfth Chapter) shows the descent of the hereditary mayors of the family of Pepin of Landen, who were the ancestors of the Carolingian Franks. Landen is a town of Liège in Belgium, close to the present border of Brabant, and about thirty miles due west of Tongres.

Siegbert of Austria died in the year 656, and Erkinoald, who was then Mayor of Neustria, succeeded in making Clovis II, and after him his son Clotair III., sole king of the Franks.^ When Erkinoald died in 657, Ebroin was elected Mayor by the Neustrian vote. But the union of the kingdoms did not long remain firm, for in 660 the Austrians demanded that Childeric, second son of Clovis, should be sent to Metz, and Wulfoald was elected Mayor. Ebroin made violent struggles to maintain his position, until he was finally slain in 681.

In 673 the Austrians recalled Dagobert from Ireland, and made him king. He was disinclined to play the part of *roi faineant*, and an insurrection, headed by Pepin of Héristal, the nephew of Grimoald, and his cousin, Duke Martin, ended in his death. In 679 the Merovingian monarchy virtually disappeared from Eastern Francia. From the year just mentioned Austria was governed by an aristocracy headed by the cousins, of whom Martin, however, was slain in the next struggle with Neustria. Pepin had better fortune, and, after the death of Ebroin, he practically ruled both countries. He continued to recognize Theodoric as king, while taking on himself the government of Neustria, the control of the royal treasures, and the supreme command of the army.

Under the title of Mayor of the Palace he governed until his death in 714. After this event, Neustria broke into open revolt Pepin of Héristal's widow, Pletruda, cast his natural son Charles (Martel) into a dungeon, and set out for Neustria with a force drawn from the *leudes* of Pepin and Grimoald, apparently designing to govern under cover of the name of the young Dagobert III. The Neustrians, however, cut this force to pieces, and the Austrians were for a time in great danger. Charles, fortunately for them, managed to escape from his prison, and rallied round him the Austrian army, with whose aid in 717-9 he utterly crushed the Neustrians, and was then recognised as Duke of Austria. According to Fredegarius he had enthroned Clotair IV., of whose parentage we are ignorant, and who did not survive the fourth year of his nominal reign at Metz.

Charles began at an early age to display those qualities of impetuosity and sustained force, both in fighting and in the exercise of government, that were to earn for him the title of Martel. He never accepted defeat, but, like his grandson after him, struck again and again until his purpose was accomplished. Scarcely had he triumphed over the Neustrians when it became necessary for him to turn his attention to his German neighbours on the east. Still maintaining the hereditary Merovingian puppet on the throne — Theodoric IV., a boy of seven, succeeding Chilperic II of Neustria in 720 — he played in every other respect the part of king, and in particular led the armies of the Franks to victory against their enemies. Saxons, Bavarians, and Allemans successively felt the weight of his heavy hand. Fresh troubles arose and were quelled in Neustria. Aquitaine, never yet wholly restful under the sway of its conquerors, defied the son of Pepin more or less openly for several years. In the Frisian lands, in Burgundy and Provence, this greatest of the Mayors reasserted the supremacy of the Franks, and confirmed the power which the effete Merovingians were no longer able to wield.

But the crowning triumph of Charles Martel was gained over the encroaching Saracens, who in 730 began to pour into Aquitaine, and who soon overran Gascony and Septimania. Odo, the Duke of Aquitaine, was now only too glad to appeal to the warlike Mayor of Austria. Charles led an army across the Loire, and found the Saracens advanced as far as the plain country lying to the north of Poitiers. Here, in October, 732, he overthrew them in a famous victory, and turned the tide of infidel conquest in Western Europe. The Saracens fled southwards again, but they continued to hold

Avignon, Narbonne, and other towns on the Mediterranean seaboard. As soon as Charles had settled other difficulties on the north and east of the Austrian kingdom, he marched once more against the Moslems, took Avignon in 737, and drove the Saracens from the neighbourhood of Narbonne.

He was now the acknowledged champion of Christendom, and Gregory III sent an embassy from Rome, soliciting his aid against the Lombards. It cannot, however, be said that Charles was popular in his character as a champion. He levied toll of those whom he assisted, as conquerors have frequently found themselves compelled to do; and his *leudes* are said to have been enriched at the expense of the Church.

Both Pepin of Héristal and his warlike son renewed the attempt of Dagobert to subdue and Christianize the Frisians. Charles Martel so far succeeded that Radbod, the Frisian duke, consented to undergo the rite of baptism. But Radbod admitted a qualm of conscience at a fatal moment. Standing with one foot in the font, he suddenly turned round to the presiding bishop, Wolfran, and said, "Where are my ancestors who have gone before me?" "They are in hell," said Wolfran, "with other infidels." "Good," said Radbod, as he withdrew from the water; "I had rather feast with my forefathers in the halls of Woden than live in heaven with those fasting little Christians of yours." The chance was gone, and Charles had to do his fighting over again. He defeated Poppo, the son of Radbod, in 750; but it remained for Charles the Great to bring the double work of subjugation to an end.

Charles was not destined to see Rome, nor yet to work out the problem of kingship in Austria. He died in his fifty-second year (741), leaving three sons, Carloman, Pepin, and Grippo. During the next few years Carloman and Pepin signalised their accession to the government of Austria and Neustria by repeating the achievements of their father in Allemania, Bavaria, Saxony, and Aquitaine; whilst Childeric III — another puppet of unknown parentage, the last of his family — had been brought from a convent and crowned king of Austria.

In 747 Carloman assumed the cowl, and the authority of Pepin (distinguished from others of his name as Pepin le Bref, owing to the shortness of his stature) was recognized throughout the Frank dominions.

It has been suggested by some writers, though on insufficient evidence, that Childebrand, the younger brother of Charles Martel, was the ancestor of Hugues Capet, the first King of France.

In 752 Pepin considered that the fitting moment had arrived for setting the crown of Francia on his head. Childeric was of so little account in his kingdom that no strong opposition was to be feared from him or his friends; but there was more reason to hesitate over the jealousy which might be aroused on the part of the Frank aristocracy. It is possible that encouragement had already been given to the ambition of Pepin by the ecclesiastics, by the memory of Pope Gregory's appeal to his father, and by the growing perplexities of Pope Stephen. At any rate the last of the Mayors could reckon on the powerful influence of the Church. And so the fateful step was taken; Childeric was hustled off to another convent, and Pepin became King of the Franks.

We may note, before concluding this chapter, what Sismondi has to say in his "History of the French" concerning the origin of the Mayors. Fredegarius, or a writer to whom this name has been given, speaks of the election of a Mayor during the minority of Siegbert I; but, as Siegbert was never a minor, Sismondi concludes that the chronicler was thinking of Childebert II (561-75), and that at any rate he is to be trusted as proving that the Franks, not later than 575, elected their own officers to represent their interests at the court of the king. "The nation sometimes dispensed with the election, but, when it did nominate a Mayor, it was for the purpose of subjecting the nobles to discipline," when the king was not yet, or no longer, able to control them.

Sismondi goes on to say that "a name translated from one language to another has been the cause of a long-lived error about the functions of this officer." He believes that a confusion arose, and was allowed to grow up, between the "mord-dom," or judge in cases of murder, and the "Major Domus," or chief domestic officer of the court Gregory, in fact, calls Waddon, manifestly an officer of the latter kind, major domus. Bandegisil, bishop of Le Mans from 581 to 586, is also named in Gregory's chronicle under the same title, though he would certainly not have been elected by the Franks to control the *leudes*.

The fact remains that, as early as the sixth century, the title of Major Domus was given to the controlling, popularly elected officers — to the officer mentioned by Fredegarius, to Duke Wintrion or Quintrion, elected after the death of Chilperic of Soissons, in 584, and to a similar officer elected by the Burgundians after the death of Gontran, nine years later.

www.ingramcontent.com/pod-product-compliance
Lightning Source LLC
Chambersburg PA
CBHW031400040426
42444CB00005B/361